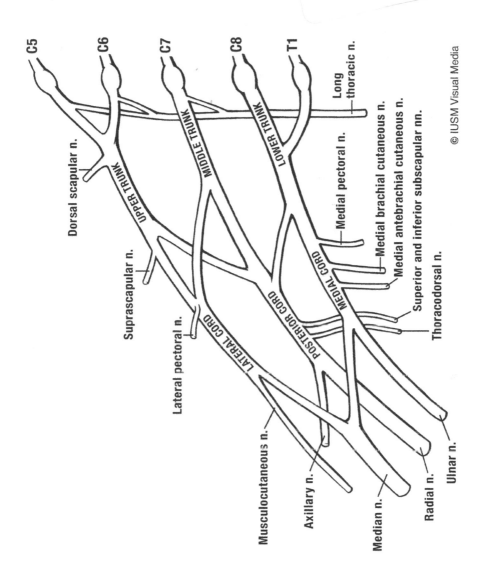

C5
C6
C7
C8
T1

Dorsal scapular n.

UPPER TRUNK

MIDDLE TRUNK

LOWER TRUNK

Long thoracic n.

Suprascapular n.

POSTERIOR CORD

MEDIAL CORD

Medial pectoral n.

Medial brachial cutaneous n.

Medial antebrachial cutaneous n.

Superior and inferior subscapular nn.

Thoracodorsal n.

Lateral pectoral n.

LATERAL CORD

Musculocutaneous n.

Axillary n.

Median n.

Radial n.

Ulnar n.

© IUSM Visual Media

BUSCHBACHER'S MANUAL OF NERVE CONDUCTION STUDIES

THIRD EDITION

BMA

BUSCHBACHER'S MANUAL OF NERVE CONDUCTION STUDIES

THIRD EDITION

Dinesh Kumbhare, MD, MSc

Associate Professor
Division of Physical Medicine
and Rehabilitation
University of Toronto
Toronto, Ontario, Canada

Lawrence Robinson, MD

Professor and Director
Division of Physical Medicine
and Rehabilitation
University of Toronto
Toronto, Ontario, Canada

Ralph Buschbacher, MD

Professor
Department of Physical Medicine
and Rehabilitation
Indiana University School of Medicine
Indianapolis, Indiana

demosMEDICAL
New York

Visit our website at www.demosmedical.com

ISBN: 9781620700877
e-book ISBN: 9781617052637

Acquisitions Editor: Beth Barry
Compositor: diacriTech

Medicine is an ever-changing science. Research and clinical experience are continually expanding our knowledge, in particular our understanding of proper treatment and drug therapy. The authors, editors, and publisher have made every effort to ensure that all information in this book is in accordance with the state of knowledge at the time of production of the book. Nevertheless, the authors, editors, and publisher are not responsible for errors or omissions or for any consequences from application of the information in this book and make no warranty, expressed or implied, with respect to the contents of the publication. Every reader should examine carefully the package inserts accompanying each drug and should carefully check whether the dosage schedules mentioned therein or the contraindications stated by the manufacturer differ from the statements made in this book. Such examination is particularly important with drugs that are either rarely used or have been newly released on the market.

Library of Congress Cataloging-in-Publication Data
Buschbacher, Ralph M., author.
  [Manual of nerve conduction studies]
  Buschbacher's manual of nerve conduction studies / Dinesh Kumbhare, Lawrence Robinson, Ralph Buschbacher. — Third edition.
      p. ; cm.
  Preceded by Manual of nerve conduction studies / Ralph M. Buschbacher, Nathan D. Prahlow. 2nd ed. c2006.
  Includes bibliographical references and index.
  ISBN 978-1-62070-087-7 — ISBN 978-1-61705-263-7 (eISBN)
  I. Kumbhare, Dinesh A., author. II. Robinson, Lawrence R. (Lawrence Russell), 1956– , author. III. Title. 1. Neural Conduction. 2. Electrodiagnosis—methods. 3. Muscle, Skeletal—innervation. 4. Reference Values. WL 102.7
  RC77
  616.85'6—dc23

                                                                      2015026902

Special discounts on bulk quantities of Demos Medical Publishing books are available to corporations, professional associations, pharmaceutical companies, health care organizations, and other qualifying groups. For details, please contact:

Special Sales Department
Demos Medical Publishing, LLC
11 West 42nd Street, 15th Floor, New York, NY 10036
Phone: 800-532-8663 or 212-683-0072; Fax: 212-941-7842
E-mail: specialsales@demosmedical.com

Printed in the United States of America by McNaughton & Gunn.
15 16 17 18 / 5 4 3 2 1

*To our families, our
teachers, and our patients*

CONTENTS

PREFACE

We are delighted to present this updated manual on nerve conduction studies. It has been a reference standard adopted by many electrophysiological laboratories in North America and the world. Included are "state-of-the-art" reference values derived by systematically assessing healthy control subjects. Where possible, the reference values have been based upon large sample sizes and have included analyses of a number of variables including height, weight, age, and gender. The presented values have used the best statistical techniques available as well as a one-tailed design. We believe that this most appropriately represents the healthy population.

The current edition adds to the previous editions of the book by including up-to-date systematic literature reviews of each nerve presented so that the reader will be able to refer to the most relevant information available on each topic.

The format of presentation in the various chapters allows side-to-side comparisons as well as same limb comparisons of different nerves with acceptable differences listed. We have also added appendices that cover common anomalous innervations such as the Martin–Gruber anastomosis.

This book is not intended to be an introductory text or a teaching manual. There are excellent textbooks available that cover these important areas. Our intention was to create a book that could be used at the bedside as a reference, used to quickly review how to perform a nerve conduction study, or to look up reference values that have not been committed to memory. We have emphasized clinical utility when developing the format of this book. This edition offers a comprehensive, up-to-date set of reference values for clinical use. By following the described techniques, the user—trainee or clinician—will have reference values that can be used with confidence.

Dinesh Kumbhare, MD, MSc
Lawrence Robinson, MD
Ralph Buschbacher, MD

INTRODUCTION

In training, residents and fellows often work at different EMG laboratories, which invariably have their own set of normal (reference) values. Discussions about how to derive these laboratory normal values typically raise many theories and suggestions, but generate little in the way of useful, practical guidance. The questions of how many normal subjects to study, which methods to use, and what machine and filter settings are most appropriate all must be considered. The unknown influence of factors such as temperature, age, height, and gender must be considered. Finally, the statistical analysis of the data must be thoughtfully completed, with the goal of producing appropriate normal values which take into account the distribution of the data.

These tasks are daunting at best, and frustratingly difficult or impossible at worst, especially in a smaller lab. Yet every EMG laboratory has to use some set of normal values, whether developed internally or borrowed from elsewhere.

The first edition of this manual started the process of creating a state-of-the-art set of normal values based on easily performed, reproducible electrographic studies of the most commonly studied nerves. These normal values were based on large populations, and were analyzed with respect to a number of variables, such as height, body mass index, age, and gender. Where the newest and largest studies were unavailable, the most appropriate study was included, whether that be based upon sample size, technique, or general 'acceptance' in the field.

Subsequent editions of this manual take up where the first left off. Many more studies are updated, replacing older studies that might have been limited by factors such as sample size, or the difficulty or reliability of technique. When possible, studies with normal values based on larger groups of subjects with varied demographics have been included. Side-to-side and same-limb comparisons of different nerves are often included, with the acceptable differences listed in the appropriate chapters.

Included for reference is a schematic of the brachial plexus inside the front cover, to be used as an aid in determining which nerves to study in complex cases.

As in the second edition, the results are presented with the mean, standard deviation, the range, and the upper or lower limit of normal. While the upper and lower limits of normal have traditionally been defined as the mean ± 2 SD, the 97th and 3rd percentiles of observed values are more appropriate when the distribution is not a bell-shaped curve (which is more commonly the case). Therefore, we have included these values when possible. In studies with smaller numbers of subjects, or when researchers have not provided the 97th/3rd percentile data, we include the mean ± 2 SD values as the upper and lower limits of normal. For rare cases, authors may use a different method of deriving the normal ranges, and these are noted when they occur.

Care should be taken that the study technique is accurately reproduced when using these normal values. Differences in technique may not seem material at first, but could yield results that lead to a patient being diagnosed inappropriately. For most studies in this book, common machine settings and techniques were used. However, in some special cases nonstandard techniques are presented. For these studies, the reader is cautioned to use the exact technique specified, in order to make the results valid.

BUSCHBACHER'S MANUAL OF NERVE CONDUCTION STUDIES

THIRD EDITION

CHAPTER 1

UPPER LIMB/BRACHIAL PLEXUS MOTOR NERVE STUDIES

AXILLARY MOTOR NERVE TO THE DELTOID

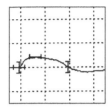

Typical waveform
appearance

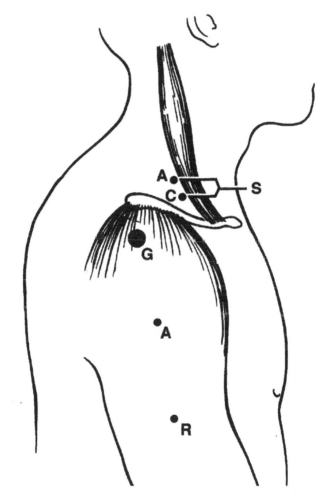

Electrode Placement

Position: This study is performed in the seated position.

Active electrode (A): Placement is over the most prominent portion of the middle deltoid.

Reference electrode (R): Placement is over the junction of the deltoid muscle and its tendon of insertion.

Ground electrode (G): Placement is on the acromion.

Stimulation point (S): Erb's point—the cathode (C) is placed slightly above the upper margin of the clavicle lateral to the clavicular head of the sternocleidomastoid muscle. The anode (A) is superomedial.

Machine settings: Sensitivity—5 mV/division, Low frequency filter—2 to 3 Hz, High frequency filter—10 kHz, Sweep speed—2 msec/division.

Nerve fibers tested: C5 and C6 nerve roots, through the upper trunk, posterior division, and posterior cord of the brachial plexus.

Reference values (1) (100 subjects) (temperature greater than or equal to 32°C) (Upper and Lower Reference values given as 97 and 3 percentile values, respectively):

Onset latency (msec)

Height in cm (in)	Mean	SD	Range	Upper Reference Value
≤170 (5'7")	4.1	0.4	3.1–4.9	4.8
>170 (5'7")	4.6	0.5	3.9–5.6	5.5
All subjects	4.3	0.5	3.1–5.6	5.4

Amplitude (mV): The data are divided into groups according to sex and body mass index (BMI), kg/m² (see Appendix 2).

Sex	BMI	Mean	SD	Range	Lower Reference Value
Male	≤30	11.0	3.7	5.1–20.2	6.2
Male	>30	9.1	3.7	3.3–14.9	3.3
Female		9.1	2.3	4.1–14.5	4.5
All subjects		9.9	3.3	3.3–20.2	4.6

Area of negative phase (mVms)

Mean	SD	Range	Lower Reference Value
62.8	20.6	20.8–130.8	27.3

Duration of negative phase (msec)

Mean	SD	Range	Upper Reference Value
9.1	1.0	6.3–11.7	10.8

Acceptable Differences

The upper limit of normal increase in latency from one side to the other is 0.5 msec.

The upper limit of normal decrease in amplitude from one side to the other is 54%.

Helpful Hints

- The active electrode is placed over the region of greatest muscle mass, localized upon abduction of the shoulder.

- Be aware that stimulation often also activates the biceps and brachialis, which can conduct volume to the recording electrodes.

Notes

REFERENCE

1. Buschbacher RM, Weir SK, Bentley JR, et al. Motor nerve conduction studies using surface electrode recording from supraspinatus, infraspinatus, deltoid, and biceps. *PM&R*. 2009;1:101–106.

ADDITIONAL READINGS

Dimberg EL. Electrodiagnostic evaluation of ulnar neuropathy and other upper extremity mononeuropathies. *Neurol Clin*. 2012;30(2):479–503.

Gassel MM. A test of nerve conduction to muscles of the shoulder girdle as an aid in the diagnosis of proximal neurogenic and muscular disease. *J Neurol Neurosurg Psychiatry*. 1964;27:200–205.

Kraft GH. Axillary, musculocutaneous and suprascapular nerve latency studies. *Arch Phys Med Rehabil*. 1972;53:383–387.

LONG THORACIC MOTOR NERVE TO THE SERRATUS ANTERIOR

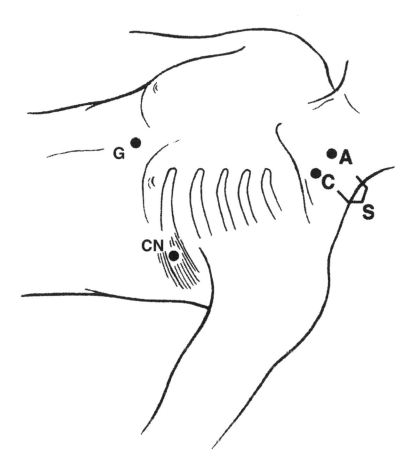

Electrode Placement

Recording electrodes: A concentric needle (CN) electrode is placed at the digitation of the serratus anterior along the midaxillary line over the 5th rib (1). Alternately, a monopolar needle electrode can be placed in this same site, with the reference electrode 2 cm caudal and the ground electrode at the anterior axillary line over the 12th rib level (2).

Stimulation point (S): Erb's point—the cathode (C) is placed slightly above the upper margin of the clavicle lateral to the clavicular head of the sternocleidomastoid muscle. The anode (A) is superomedial.

Machine settings: Standard motor settings are used.

Nerve fibers tested: Anterior primary branches of the C5, C6, and C7 nerve roots, and the long thoracic nerve.

Reference values:

Onset latency (1) (msec—44 subjects, concentric needle recording)

Age Range	Mean	SD	Upper Reference Value
20–35	3.6	0.3	4.2
36–50	3.8	0.4	4.6
51–65	4.0	0.4	4.8

Onset latency (2) (msec—25 subjects, monopolar needle recording, room temperature 21°C to 23°C)

Mean	SD	Upper Reference Value
3.9	0.6	5.1

Helpful Hints

- In the study by Alfonsi and colleagues (1) the mean distance between stimulating and recording electrodes was 23.6 ± 1 cm, measured with obstetric calipers (range 22–25 cm). The latency was found to correlate with distance, with approximately a 0.2 msec increase in latency for each 1 cm increase in distance. In Kaplan's study (2), the distances ranged from 17 to 23 cm.

- Surface recording techniques have also been described (1,3,4). Ma and Liveson (3) studied 15 subjects and placed the active electrode over the midaxillary line of the 5th or 6th ribs with the reference electrode at the anterior axillary line of the same rib, and reported a latency of 3.0 ± 0.2 msec. Alfonsi and coworkers (1) utilized surface recording but they concluded that these recordings may be contaminated by volume conduction from other muscles and recommended using a needle recording technique. Cherrington (4) also studied this nerve using surface recording in 20 normal subjects. Stimulation was applied at Erb's point and recording was just lateral to the nipple. Normal latencies ranged from 2.6 to 4.0 msec over a distance of 18.0 to 22.0 cm.

- Proper needle placement can be confirmed with active protraction.

- If the recording electrode is placed too far posteriorly, it may result in erroneous recording from the latissimus dorsi.

Notes

REFERENCES

1. Alfonsi E, Moglia A, Sandrini G, et al. Electrophysiological study of long thoracic nerve conduction in normal subjects. *Electromyogr clin Neurophysiol.* 1986;26:63–67.
2. Kaplan PE. Electrodiagnostic confirmation of long thoracic palsy. *J Neurol Neurosurg Psychiatry.* 1980;43:50–52.

3. Ma DM, Liveson JA. *Nerve Conduction Handbook*. Philadelphia, PA: FA Davis; 1983.
4. Cherrington M. Long thoracic nerve: conduction studies. *Dis Nerv Syst*. 1972;33:49–51.

ADDITIONAL READING/ALTERNATE TECHNIQUE

LoMonaco M, DiPasqua PG, Tonali P. Conduction studies along the accessory, long thoracic, dorsal scapular, and thoracodorsal nerves. *Acta Neurol Scand*. 1983;68:171–176.

MEDIAN NERVE

MEDIAN MOTOR NERVE TO THE ABDUCTOR POLLICIS BREVIS

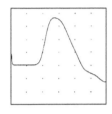

Typical waveform
appearance

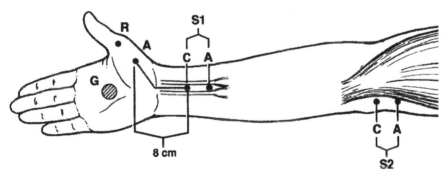

Electrode Placement

Position: This study is performed in the supine position.

Active electrode (A): Placement is halfway between the midpoint of the distal wrist crease and the first metacarpophalangeal (MCP) joint.

Reference electrode (R): Placement is slightly distal to the first MCP joint.

Ground electrode (G): Placement is on the dorsum of the hand. If stimulus artifact interferes with the recording, the ground may be placed near the active electrode, between this electrode and the cathode.

Stimulation point 1 (S1): The cathode (C) is placed 8 cm proximal to the active electrode, in a line measured first to the midpoint of the distal wrist crease and then to a point slightly ulnar to the tendon of the flexor carpi radialis. The anode (A) is proximal.

Stimulation point 2 (S2): The cathode (C) is placed slightly medial to the brachial artery pulse in the antecubital region. The anode (A) is proximal.

F-wave stimulation: The cathode (C) is positioned as for stimulation point 1, but with the anode distal.

Machine settings: Sensitivity—5 mV/division, Low frequency filter—2 to 3 Hz, High frequency filter—10 kHz, Sweep speed—2 msec/division.

Nerve fibers tested: C8 and T1 nerve roots, through the lower trunk, anterior division, and medial cord of the brachial plexus.

Reference values (1) (249 subjects) (skin temperature over the dorsum of the hand greater than or equal to 32°C):

Onset latency (msec)

		Males		
Age Range	*Mean*	*SD*	*Range*	*Upper Reference Value*
19–49	3.8	0.4	3.0–4.6	4.6
50–79	4.0	0.4	3.0–4.8	4.7
		Females		
Age Range	*Mean*	*SD*	*Range*	*Upper Reference Value*
19–49	3.5	0.4	2.8–4.8	4.4
50–79	3.8	0.4	2.9–4.6	4.4
All subjects	3.7	0.5	2.8–4.8	4.5

Amplitude (mV)

Age Range	Mean	SD	Range	Lower Reference Value
19–39	11.9	3.6	2.2–22.0	5.9
40–59	9.8	2.8	3.3–17.7	4.2
60–79	7.0	2.6	2.0–14.3	3.8
All subjects	10.2	3.6	2.0–22.0	4.1

Area of negative phase (mVms)

Age Range	Mean	SD	Range	Lower Reference Value
19–49	37.4	12.9	8.1–93.7	14.6
50–59	30.9	8.6	14.1–45.6	15.3
60–79	23.7	9.3	6.6–50.9	11.9
All subjects	33.7	12.8	6.6–93.7	12.4

Duration of negative phase (msec)

Age Range	Mean	SD	Range	Upper Reference Value
19–79	5.9	0.9	4.1–9.6	8.0

Nerve conduction velocity (m/sec)

		Males		
Age Range	Mean	SD	Range	Lower Reference Value
19–39	58	4	48–65	49
40–79	55	5	40–78	47

		Females		
Age Range	Mean	SD	Range	Lower Reference Value
19–39	60	3	50–66	53
40–79	57	5	43–77	51
All subjects	57	5	40–78	49

F-wave latencies (msec) (2) (195 subjects)—shortest of 10 stimuli

		Age Range 19–49		
Height in cm (in)	Mean	SD	Range	Upper Reference Value
<160 (5'3")	23.7	1.0	22.7–25.4	25.7
160–169 (5'3"–5'6")	25.3	1.6	21.4–30.0	28.5
170–179 (5'7"–5'10")	27.3	1.8	23.7–31.0	30.9
≥180 (5'11")	28.9	2.3	26.0–34.3	33.5

Age Range 50–79

Height in cm (in)				
<160 (5'3")	25.2	1.7	21.0–27.6	28.6
160–169 (5'3"–5'6")	27.5	1.4	25.5–30.5	30.3
170–179 (5'7"–5'10")	28.7	1.4	25.9–31.3	31.5
≥180 (5'11")	30.4	1.9	26.5–33.0	34.2
All subjects	26.8	2.4	21.0–34.3	31.6

Acceptable Differences

The upper limit of normal increase in latency from one side to the other is 0.7 msec.

The upper limit of normal decrease in amplitude from one side to the other is 54%.

The upper limit of normal decrease in nerve conduction velocity from one side to the other is 9 m/sec.

The upper limit of normal decrease in amplitude from wrist to elbow stimulation is 24%.

The upper limit of normal side to side difference in the shortest F-wave latency is 2.2 msec.

The upper limit of normal difference between median (digit 3) and ulnar (digit 5) motor latency in the same limb is 1.4 msec (ages 19–49), 1.7 msec (ages 50–79), and 1.5 msec (all subjects) in cases where the median has the longer latency; it is 0.0 msec (ages 19–49), –0.3 msec (ages 50–79), and 0.0 msec (all subjects) in cases where the ulnar latency is longer (3).

Helpful Hints

- Care should be taken to not concomitantly stimulate the ulnar nerve. The direction of thumb twitch will help in making sure that only the median nerve is stimulated. In addition to observing the twitch while stimulating the waveforms, the deflections from baseline and their shape should especially be monitored for change in shape. The waveforms should be similar on proximal and distal stimulation.

- Stimulation can also be performed at the palm. This technique stimulates the second lumbrical and interossei muscles. If the amplitude with palm stimulation is significantly greater than with wrist stimulation, this can be a sign of neurapraxia at the wrist (4,5). Pease and coworkers (6) showed that the increase in amplitude with wrist stimulation is significantly larger in persons with carpal tunnel syndrome than in normal controls. Proximal to distal amplitude ratios of 0.5 to 0.8 have been recommended as the limits of normality (5,7). The 0.5 value is more conservative, reduces the possibility of false positives, and seems reasonable for clinical use. Anatomically, it is known that the fibers from the median nerve to the second lumbrical are relatively spared as compared to those supplying the thenar eminence a lumbrical response may be obtained in severe median mononeuropathy when the compound muscle action potential (CMAP) recorded from the abductor pollicis brevis (APB) is absent (1,8,9).

- Midpalmar stimulation may cause a direct excitation of the thenar muscle mass or of the deep branch of the ulnar nerve. Please keep in mind that the ulnar nerve can supply a component of the thenar muscle mass (4,8,10). It is helpful to move the cathode slightly distally on the palm and stimulate the patient a few times while repositioning the cathode gradually more proximal, to optimize the resultant waveform recording. Stimulus artifact can be a problem and may be minimized by rotating the anode about the cathode and stimulating at various locations. Because the skin of the palm is thick, a longer pulse duration may be needed. Needle stimulation may be necessary in some cases.

- More proximal stimulation can also be performed at the axilla and at Erb's point in the supraclavicular fossa. This can allow determination of waveform changes across more proximal segments of the nerve and calculation of more proximal nerve conduction velocity. When calculating the conduction velocity of the Erb's point-to-axilla segment, obstetric calipers are used to measure the distance.

- Anomalous innervation due to a Martin–Gruber (median to ulnar) anastomosis in the forearm is common, although it is less commonly clinically significant during electrodiagnostic studies. When present in a patient with carpal tunnel syndrome, it may cause confusion. For instance, a complete block of the median nerve to wrist stimulation may seem to be reversed on elbow stimulation. Martin–Gruber anastomosis should be suspected if the median motor amplitude is larger on elbow stimulation than on wrist stimulation, and in persons with median nerve slowing across the wrist who have a higher than normal conduction velocity across the forearm. It should also be suspected if proximal (but not distal) median nerve stimulation results in an initially positive deflection.

Martin–Gruber anastomosis can usually be confirmed by repositioning the active electrode to the first dorsal interosseous muscle. Stimulation of the median nerve at the elbow, but not the wrist, results in a negative deflection. Stimulation at the elbow should also result in a significantly larger amplitude response than with wrist stimulation (10). An accurate forearm conduction velocity cannot be calculated in the person with carpal tunnel syndrome and a Martin–Gruber anastomosis.

Martin–Gruber anastomosis is described in detail in Appendix 1.

Notes _____

REFERENCES

1. Buschbacher RM. Median nerve motor conduction to the abductor pollicis brevis. *Am J Phys Med Rehabil*. 1999;78:S1–S8.
2. Buschbacher RM. Median nerve F-waves. *Am J Phys Med Rehabil*. 1999;78:S32–S37.
3. Grossart EA, Prahlow ND, Buschbacher RM. Acceptable differences in sensory and motor latencies between the median and ulnar nerves. *J Long-term Eff Med Implants*. 2006;16(5):395–400.
4. Preston DC, Ross MH, Kothari MJ, et al. The median–ulnar latency difference studies are comparable in mild carpal tunnel syndrome. *Muscle Nerve*. 1994;17:1469–1471.
5. Ross MA, Kimura J. AAEM case report #2: the carpal tunnel syndrome. *Muscle Nerve*. 1995;18:567–573.
6. Pease WS, Cunningham ML, Walsh WE, Johnson EW. Determining neurapraxia in carpal tunnel syndrome. *Am J Phys Med Rehabil*. 1988;67:117–119.
7. Fitz WR, Mysiw J, Johnson EW. First lumbrical latency and amplitude: control values and findings in carpal tunnel syndrome. *Am J Phys Med Rehabil*. 1990;69:198–201.
8. Lesser EA, Venkatesh S, Preston DC, Logigian EL. Stimulation distal to the lesion in patients with carpal tunnel syndrome. *Muscle Nerve*. 1995;18:503–507.
9. Preston DC, Logigian EL. Lumbrical and interossei recording in carpal tunnel syndrome. *Muscle Nerve*. 1992;15:1253–1257.
10. Sun SF, Streib EW. Martin-Gruber anastomosis: electromyographic studies. *Electromyogr clin Neurophysiol*. 1983;23:271–285.

ADDITIONAL READINGS

American Association of Electrodiagnostic Medicine, American Academy of Neurology, American Academy of Physical Medicine & Rehabilitation. Practice parameter for electrodiagnostic studies in carpal tunnel syndrome: summary statement. *Muscle Nerve*. 2002;25:918–922.

Chang MH, Wei SJ, Chiang HL, et al. Comparison of motor conduction techniques in the diagnosis of carpal tunnel syndrome. *Neurology*. 2002;58(11):1603–1607.

D'Arcy CA, McGee S. The rational clinical examination. Does this patient have carpal tunnel syndrome? *JAMA*. 2000;283(23):3110–3117.

Falco FJE, Hennessey WJ, Braddom RL, Goldberg G. Standardized nerve conduction studies in the upper limb of the healthy elderly. *Am J Phys Med Rehabil*. 1992;71:263–271.

Gazioglu S, Boz C, Cakmak VA. Electrodiagnosis of carpal tunnel syndrome in patients with diabetic polyneuropathy. *Clin Neurophysiol*. 2011;122(7):1463–1469.

Position: This study is performed in the supine position.

Active electrode (A): Placement is over the belly of the flexor carpi radialis, one-third of the distance from the medial epicondyle to the radial styloid.

Reference electrode (R): Placement is over the radial styloid.

Ground electrode (G): Placement is on the dorsum of the hand.

Stimulation point (S): 10 cm proximal to the active electrode, over the median nerve in the antecubital area. The anode is proximal.

Machine settings: Sensitivity—5 mV/division, Low frequency filter—2 to 3 Hz, High frequency filter—10 kHz, Sweep speed—2 msec/division.

Nerve fibers tested: C6, C7, and C8 nerve roots, through the upper, middle, and lower trunks, anterior divisions, and the medial and lateral cords of the brachial plexus.

Reference values (1) (208 subjects) (skin temperature over the dorsum of the hand greater than or equal to 32°C):

Onset latency (msec)

Mean	SD	Range	Upper Reference Value
2.8	0.4	2.1–3.8	3.6

Amplitude (mV)

Age Range	Mean	SD	Range	Lower Reference Value
19–49	11.5	3.4	1.9–18.2	3.0
50–79	8.3	4.0	1.5–22.4	1.7
All subjects	10.2	4.0	1.5–22.4	2.3

Area of negative phase (mVms)

Age Range	Mean	SD	Range	Lower Reference Value
19–49	66.8	19.7	11.0–107.0	15.5
50–79	48.4	21.3	5.3–119.0	6.9
All subjects	59.0	22.3	5.3–119.0	12.9

Duration of negative phase (msec)

Mean	SD	Range	Upper Reference Value
9.7	1.2	6.1–13.1	11.8

Acceptable Differences

The upper limit of normal increase in latency from one side to the other is 0.8 msec.

The upper limit of normal decrease in amplitude from one side to the other is 53%.

The upper limit of normal difference between pronator teres and flexor carpi radialis latency in the same limb is 0.8 msec in cases where the pronator teres has the longer latency; it is 0.4 msec in cases where the flexor carpi radialis latency is longer.

Notes

REFERENCE

1. Foley BS, Buschbacher RM. Establishing normal values of the proximal median motor nerve: a study of the pronator teres and flexor carpi radialis in healthy volunteers. *J Long Term Eff Med Implants*. 2006;16(5):341–348.

ADDITIONAL READINGS

Jabre JF. Surface recording of the H-reflex of the flexor carpi radialis. *Muscle Nerve*. 1981;4:435–438.

Zheng C, Zhu Y, Lv F, et al. Abnormal flexor carpi radialis h-reflex as a specific indicator of c7 as compared with c6 radiculopathy. *J Clin Neurophysiol*. 2014;31(6):529–534.

MEDIAN MOTOR NERVE (ANTERIOR INTEROSSEOUS BRANCH) TO THE PRONATOR QUADRATUS

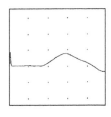

Typical waveform appearance

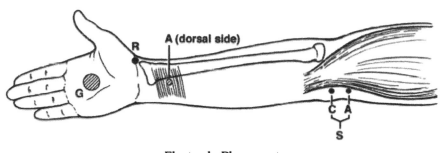

Electrode Placement

Position: This study is performed in the supine position.

Active electrode (A): Placement is at the midpoint between the radius and ulna on the dorsal forearm, 3 cm proximal to the ulnar styloid. After an adequate waveform has been obtained, the distance between cathode and active electrode is measured with calipers. The caliper distance should be measured on a ruler, as caliper calibration is often erroneous. The caliper measurement may be transferred to the other limb for comparison study.

Reference electrode (R): Placement is over the radial styloid.

Ground electrode (G): Placement is on the dorsum of the hand.

Stimulation point (S): The cathode (C) is placed at the elbow, slightly medial to the brachial pulse. The anode (A) is proximal.

Machine settings: Sensitivity—5 mV/division, Low frequency filter—2 to 3 Hz, High frequency filter—10 kHz, Sweep speed—2 msec/division.

Nerve fibers tested: C7, C8, and T1 nerve roots, through the middle and lower trunks, anterior divisions, and medial and lateral cords of the brachial plexus.

Reference values (1) (207 subjects) (skin temperatures over the dorsum of the hand greater than or equal to 32°C):

Onset latency (msec)

Forearm Distance	Mean	SD	Range	Upper Reference Value
≤23 cm	3.8	0.4	3.1–4.4	4.4
23.5–24.5 cm	4.0	0.4	3.5–5.1	4.8
≥25 cm	4.5	0.4	3.7–5.3	5.2
All subjects	4.2	0.5	3.1–5.3	5.1

Amplitude (mV)

Age Range	Mean	SD	Range	Lower Reference Value
19–59	4.4	1.8	1.1–18.7	1.6
60–79	3.7	1.7	1.2–12.2	1.6
All subjects	4.3	1.8	1.1-18.7	1.6

Area of negative phase (mVms)

Age Range	Mean	SD	Range	Lower Reference Value
19–59	17.1	6.0	2.9–34.9	6.0
60–79	13.7	5.4	2.9–30.2	6.0
All subjects	16.4	6.1	2.9–34.9	6.0

Duration of negative phase (msec)

Mean	SD	Range	Upper Reference Value
7.2	1.1	4.2–12.0	9.3

Acceptable Differences

The upper limit of normal increase in latency from one side to the other is 0.6 msec.

The upper limit of normal decrease in amplitude from one side to the other is 37%.

Same-limb upper limit of normal difference for pronator quadratus minus flexor carpi radialis latencies are 2.0 msec (≤23 cm), 2.0 msec (23.5–24.5 cm), 2.4 msec (≥25 cm), and 2.2 msec (all subjects).

Same-limb upper limit of normal difference for pronator quadratus minus pronator teres latencies are 1.7 msec (≤23 cm), 1.7 msec (23.5–24.5 cm), 2.2 msec (≥25 cm), and 2.2 msec (all subjects).

Helpful Hints

- A needle recording technique has also been described (2), but Shafshak and El-Hinawy (3), who compared the two techniques, thought that the surface recording technique was more sensitive to pathology than was the needle recording technique.

- There are two heads of the pronator quadratus, which may result in a bimodal evoked response. This may limit the usefulness of the duration measurement.

Notes _____

_____

_____

_____

_____

_____

_____

_____

_____

_____

_____

_____

REFERENCES

1. Foley BS, Roslonski E, Buschbacher RM. Reference values for median nerve conduction to the pronator quadratus. *Arch Phys Med Rehabil*. 2006;87(1):88–90.
2. Nakano KK, Lundergan C, Okihiro MM. Anterior interosseous nerve syndromes: diagnostic methods and alternative treatments. *Arch Neurol*. 1977;34:477–480.
3. Shafshak TS, El-Hinaway YM. The anterior interosseous nerve latency in the diagnosis of severe carpal tunnel syndrome with unobtainable median nerve distal conduction. *Arch Phys Med Rehabil*. 1995;76:471–475.

ADDITIONAL READING

Mysiw WJ, Colachis SC. Electrophysiologic study of the anterior interosseous nerve. *Am J Phys Med Rehabil* 1988;67:50–54.

MEDIAN MOTOR NERVE TO THE PRONATOR TERES

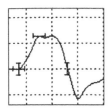

Typical waveform
appearance

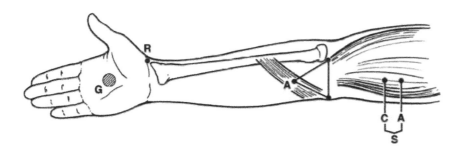

Electrode Placement

Position: This study is performed in the supine position.

Active electrode (A): An equilateral triangle is imagined, with the medial epicondyle and the biceps tendon (at the level of the epicondyle) as two of its points. The active electrode is placed at the third point, on the proximal forearm.

Reference electrode (R): Placement is over the radial styloid.

Ground electrode (G): Placement is on the dorsum of the hand.

Stimulation point (S): 10 cm proximal to the active electrode, over the median nerve in the antecubital area. The anode is proximal.

Machine settings: Sensitivity—5 mV/division, Low frequency filter—2 to 3 Hz, High frequency filter—10 kHz, Sweep speed—2 msec/division.

Nerve fibers tested: C6 and C7 nerve roots, through the upper and middle trunks, anterior divisions, and the lateral cord of the brachial plexus.

Reference values (1) (208 subjects) (skin temperature over the dorsum of the hand greater than or equal to 32°C):

Onset latency (msec)

Mean	SD	Range	Upper Reference Value
2.9	0.3	2.2–4.4	3.6

Amplitude (mV)

Age Range	Mean	SD	Range	Lower Reference Value
19–49	9.1	3.0	1.7–18.7	3.8
50–79	7.3	2.9	2.4–15.8	2.9
All subjects	8.4	3.1	1.7–18.7	2.9

Area of negative phase (mVms)

Age Range	Mean	SD	Range	Lower Reference Value
19–49	48.2	16.1	6.9–92.7	14.3
50–79	40.5	18.2	4.4–88.6	7.2
All subjects	45.1	17.4	4.4–92.7	13.2

Duration of negative phase (msec)

Mean	SD	Range	Upper Reference Value
10.0	1.4	5.4–14.0	12.5

Acceptable Differences

The upper limit of normal increase in latency from one side to the other is 0.6 msec.

The upper limit of normal decrease in amplitude from one side to the other is 54%.

The upper limit of normal difference between pronator teres and flexor carpi radialis latency in the same limb is 0.8 msec in cases where the pronator teres has the longer latency; it is 0.4 msec in cases where the flexor carpi radialis latency is longer.

Notes

REFERENCE

1. Foley BS, Buschbacher RM. Establishing normal values of the proximal median motor nerve: a study of the pronator teres and flexor carpi radialis in healthy volunteers. *J Long Term Eff Med Implants*. 2006;16(5):341–348.

ADDITIONAL READINGS

Marchini C, Marinig R, Bergonzi P. Median nerve F-wave study derived by flexor carpi radialis. *Electromyog Clin Neuro*. 1998;38(8):451–453.

Werner CO, Rosen I, Thorngren KG. Clinical and neurophysiologic characteristics of the pronator syndrome. *Clin Orthop Relat Res*. 1985;197:231–236.

MEDIAN MOTOR NERVE TO THE 1ST LUMBRICAL

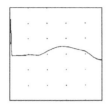

Typical waveform
appearance

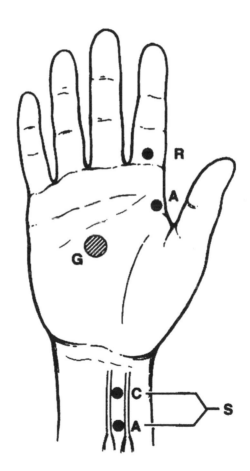

Electrode Placement

Position: This study is performed in the supine position.

Active electrode (A): Placement is on the palm, slightly radial to the long flexor tendon of the index finger (localized by flexion of the index finger) and 1 cm proximal to the midpalmar crease.

Reference electrode (R): Placement is at the base of the index finger.

Ground electrode (G): Placement is on the dorsum of the hand.

Stimulation point (S): The cathode (C) is placed 10 cm proximal to the active electrode, in a line measured first to the midpoint of the distal wrist crease and then to a point slightly ulnar to the tendon of the flexor carpi radialis. The anode (A) is proximal.

Machine settings: Sensitivity—5 mV/division, Low frequency filter—2 to 3 Hz, High frequency filter—10 kHz, Sweep speed—2 msec/division.

Nerve fibers tested: C8 and T1 nerve roots, through the lower trunk, anterior division, and medial cord of the brachial plexus.

Reference values (1) (196 subjects) (skin temperature over the dorsum of the hand greater than or equal to 32°C):

Onset latency (msec)

Mean	SD	Range	Upper Reference Value
3.6	0.4	2.7–4.8	4.4

Amplitude (mV)

Mean	SD	Range	Lower Reference Value
2.5	2.0	0.7–11.2	0.8

Area of negative phase (mVms)

Mean	SD	Range	Lower Reference Value
8.3	5.2	2.1–32.3	2.7

Duration of negative phase (msec)

Mean	SD	Range	Upper Reference Value
6.0	1.2	3.1–10.2	9.3

Acceptable Differences

The upper limit of normal increase in latency from one side to the other is 0.7 msec.

The upper limit of normal decrease in amplitude from one side to the other is 59%.

The upper limit of normal difference between 1st lumbrical and 2nd lumbrical latency in the same limb is 0.7 msec in cases where the 2nd lumbrical has the longer latency; it is 0.6 msec in cases where the 1st lumbrical latency is longer.

The upper limit of normal difference between 1st lumbrical and APB latency in the same limb is 1.0 msec in cases where the APB has the longer latency; it is 0.6 msec in cases where the 1st lumbrical latency is longer.

Helpful Hint

- Stimulation can also be performed at the palm. If the amplitude with palm stimulation is significantly greater than with wrist stimulation, this may be a sign of neurapraxia at the wrist. The upper limit of normal increase in amplitude for palm versus wrist stimulation (mean + 2 SD) is 105% (mean increase 22%, range –4% to 70%). Palmar stimulation may be difficult in persons with thick skin and may also activate other nerve branches or muscles directly. The waveform shape should be the same as with wrist stimulation (2).

Notes

_____

_____

_____

_____

REFERENCES

1. Foley BS, Buschbacher RM. Establishing normal nerve conduction values; lumbrical and interosseous responses. *J Long Term Eff Med Implants.* 2006;16(5):359–368.
2. Fitz WR, Mysiw WJ, Johnson EW. First lumbrical latency and amplitude: control values and findings in carpal tunnel syndrome. *Am J Phys Med Rehabil.* 1990;69:198–201.

MEDIAN MOTOR NERVE TO THE 2ND LUMBRICAL (*SEE ALSO* ULNAR MOTOR NERVE TO THE PALMAR INTEROSSEOUS)

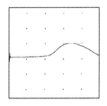

Typical waveform
appearance

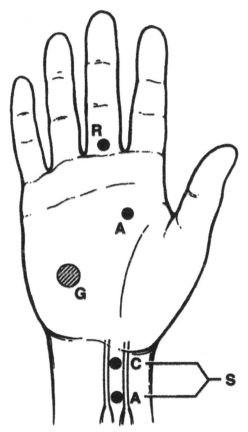

Electrode Placement

See also page 82 for the Ulnar Motor Nerve to the Palmar Interosseous.

Position: This study is performed in the supine position.

Active electrode (A): Placement is on the palm, slightly radial and proximal (1 cm) to the midpoint of the third metacarpal and the distal wrist crease.

Reference electrode (R): Placement is slightly distal to the third MCP joint.

Ground electrode (G): Placement is on the dorsum of the hand.

Stimulation point (S): The cathode (C) is placed 10 cm proximal to the active electrode, in a line measured first to the midpoint of the distal wrist crease and then to a point slightly ulnar to the tendon of the flexor carpi radialis. The anode (A) is proximal.

Machine settings: Sensitivity—2 mV/division, Low frequency filter—2 to 3 Hz, High frequency filter—10 kHz, Sweep speed—2 msec/division.

Nerve fibers tested: C8 and T1 nerve roots, through the lower trunk, anterior division, and medial cord of the brachial plexus.

Reference values (1) (196 subjects) (skin temperature over the dorsum of the hand greater than or equal to 32°C):

Onset latency (msec)

Mean	SD	Range	Upper Reference Value
3.7	0.4	2.7–5.1	4.5

Amplitude (mV)

Mean	SD	Range	Lower Reference Value
3.0	2.0	0.7–11.7	1.0

Area of negative phase (mVms)

Mean	SD	Range	Lower Reference Value
9.4	5.4	1.6–33.7	3.3

Duration of negative phase (msec)

Mean	SD	Range	Upper Reference Value
5.7	1.1	3.3–10.4	8.4

Acceptable Differences

The upper limit of normal increase in latency from one side to the other is 0.8 msec.

The upper limit of normal decrease in amplitude from one side to the other is 67%.

The upper limit of normal difference between 1st lumbrical and 2nd lumbrical latency in the same limb is 0.7 msec in cases where the 2nd lumbrical has the longer latency; it is 0.6 msec in cases where the 1st lumbrical latency is longer.

The upper limit of normal difference between 2nd lumbrical and APB latency in the same limb is 1.0 msec in cases where the APB has the longer latency; it is 0.8 msec in cases where the 2nd lumbrical latency is longer.

The upper limit of normal difference between 2nd lumbrical and interosseous latency in the same limb is 0.2 msec in cases where the interosseous has the longer latency; it is 1.2 msec in cases where the 2nd lumbrical latency is longer.

Helpful Hints

- Concomitant median and ulnar nerve stimulation must be avoided.

- Prolonged wrist flexion (2–5 minutes) can result in elevations in latency; therefore, we suggest that the median nerve study be standardized to avoid this. This can result in false positive diagnoses of median nerve mononeuropathy (2,3).

- The second lumbrical and interosseous muscles lie superimposed in this location. Stimulating the median nerve activates the lumbrical, whereas stimulating the ulnar nerve activates the interosseous muscle. Both nerve studies have approximately the same latencies and can thus be compared to detect slowing of one nerve or the other.

- Sometimes the median mixed nerve potential (pre-motor potential) is seen before the desired motor response on median nerve stimulation. This potential should be ignored and does not generally distort the measurement from the second lumbrical.

- Anomalous innervation is common and may result in no response being seen to stimulation of one of the involved nerves.

- Conduction to the lumbricals may persist in carpal tunnel syndrome even when the APB response is absent. Therefore, this technique is especially helpful in patients with severe median mononeuropathy at the wrist because a lumbrical response may be obtained when responses from the APB are absent (4–7).

Notes _____

_____

_____

_____

REFERENCES

1. Foley BS, Buschbacher RM. Establishing normal nerve conduction values; lumbrical and interosseous responses. *J Long Term Eff Med Implants.* 2006;16(5):359–368.
2. Schwartz MS, Gordon JA, Swash M. Slowed nerve conduction with wrist flexion in carpal tunnel syndrome. *Ann Neurol.* 1980;8:69–71.
3. Marin EL, Vernick S, Friedmann LW. Carpal tunnel syndrome: median nerve stress test. *Arch Phys Med Rehabil.* 1983;64:206–208.
4. Preston DC, Logigian EL. Lumbrical and interossei recording in carpal tunnel syndrome. *Muscle Nerve.* 1992;15:1253–1257.
5. Logigian EL, Busis NA, Berger AR, et al. Lumbrical sparing in carpal tunnel syndrome: anatomic, physiologic, and diagnostic implications. *Neurology.* 1987;37:1499–1505.
6. Uncini A, DiMuzio A, Awad J, et al. Sensitivity of three median-to-ulnar comparative tests in diagnosis of mild carpal tunnel syndrome. *Muscle Nerve.* 1993;16:1366–1373.
7. Löscher WN, Auer-Grumbach M, Trinka E, et al. Comparison of second lumbrical and interosseous latencies with standard measures of median nerve function across the carpal tunnel: a prospective study of 450 hands. *J Neurol.* 2000;247:530–534.

ADDITIONAL READINGS

Muellbacher W, Mamoli B, Zifko U, Grisold W. Lumbrical and interossei recording in carpal tunnel syndrome (letter to the editor). *Muscle Nerve.* 1994;17:359–360.

Seror P. The value of special motor and sensory tests for the diagnosis of benign and minor median nerve lesion at the wrist. *Am J Phys Med Rehabil.* 1995;74:124–129.

Sheean GL, Houser MK, Murray MF. Lumbrical-interosseous latency comparison in the diagnosis of carpal tunnel syndrome. *Electroencephalogr Clin Neurophysiol.* 1995;97:285–289.

H-REFLEX TO THE FLEXOR CARPI RADIALIS

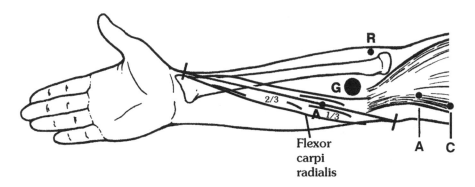

Electrode Placement

Position: This study is performed in the supine position.

Active electrode (A): Placement is over the belly of the flexor carpi radialis, usually one-third of the distance from the medial epicondyle to the radial styloid.

Reference electrode (R): Placement is over the brachioradialis.

Ground electrode (G): Placement is between the stimulating and recording electrodes.

Stimulation: The median nerve is stimulated at the elbow with a 0.5–1.0 msec rectangular pulse with a frequency not more than 0.5 Hz. The cathode (C) is proximal, and the anode (A) is distal.

Machine settings: Standard motor settings are used, with a sweep speed of 5 msec/division and a sensitivity of 500 μV/division (1,2).

Nerve fibers tested: C6, C7, and C8 nerve roots, through the upper, middle, and lower trunks, anterior divisions, and the medial and lateral cords of the brachial plexus.

Reference values (1) (39 subjects) temperature not reported. Upper and lower reference values are calculated as mean ± 2 SD:

Onset latency (msec)

Mean	SD	Upper Reference Value
15.9	1.5	18.9

Amplitude (mV, baseline to highest negative peak)

Mean	SD	Lower Reference Value
1.6	0.4	0.8

Acceptable Difference

The upper limit of normal side-to-side difference in H-reflex latency is 1.0 msec (mean + 2 SD).

Helpful Hints

- Jabre (1) states that to be accepted as an H-reflex, the response must be obtained either without an M-response or with only a small M-response preceding it; its latency must be shortened when the nerve is stimulated proximally, and its amplitude must be decreased with increasing stimulation intensity. (In the opinion of this book's authors, it may be difficult to obtain an H-reflex amplitude greater than the M-wave amplitude.)

- When using these criteria, 90% of normal subjects were found to have an elicitable H-reflex. The author reports that in none of his subjects was the H-reflex absent on only one side, but this must be interpreted with caution because of the small sample size.

- Calculation of reference values using mean ± 2 SD may produce misleading results when distributions are skewed.

- An alternate description places the reference electrode over the distal tendinous area of the forearm. The muscle can be palpated just medial to the pronator teres and can be palpated with resisted wrist flexion (2).

- From the reference values located on page 39 (Jabre (1)), the cathode was placed proximally for determining both the H-reflex and the M-wave latencies. M-wave recordings usually are made with the anode proximal.

- Kraft and Johnson (2) report that H-reflex latency is 17 ± 1.7 msec with highly variable amplitude and an upper limit of normal side-to-side difference of 0.85 msec.

- Facilitation may be necessary to obtain an H-reflex response. The elbow should be slightly flexed.

- With supramaximal stimuation, an F-wave response may be mistaken for an H-reflex. For this reason, we recommend that the starting stimulus intensity should be low; in addition, monitor the M wave amplitude rise and watch the H reflex amplitude begin to increase. When the stimulus intensity is too high the H will abruptly disappear and become the F wave.

- The H reflex has been described as an adjunct determinant for diagnosing a C7 radiculopathy (3).

Notes _____

_____

_____

_____

_____

_____

REFERENCES

1. Jabre JF. Surface recording of the H-reflex of the flexor carpi radialis. *Muscle Nerve*. 1981;4:435–438.
2. Kraft GH, Johnson EW. *Proximal Motor Nerve Conduction and Late Responses* [an AAEM workshop]. Rochester, MN: American Association of Electrodiagnostic Medicine; 1986.
3. Zheng C, Zhu Y, Lv F et al. Abnormal flexor carpi radialis H reflex as a specific indicator of C7 as compared to C6 radiculopathy. *J Clin Neurophysiol Dec.* 2014;31(6):529–534.

ADDITIONAL READINGS/ALTERNATE TECHNIQUES

Miller TA, Newall AR, Jackson DA. H-reflexes in the upper extremity and the effects of voluntary contraction. *Electromyogr Clin Neurophysiol*. 1995;35:121–128.

Ongerboer De Visser BW, Schimsheimer RJ, Hart AAM. The H-reflex of the flexor carpi radialis muscle: a study in controls and radiation-induced brachial plexus lesions. *J Neurol Neurosurg Psychiatry*. 1984;47:1098–1101.

Schimsheimer RJ, Ongerboer De Visser BW, Kemp B. The flexor carpi radialis H-reflex in lesions of the sixth and seventh cervical nerve roots. *J Neurol Neurosurg Psychiatry*. 1985;48:445–449.

Schimsheimer RJ, Ongerboer De Visser BW, Kemp B, Bour LJ. The flexor carpi radialis H–reflex in polyneuropathy: relations to conduction velocities of the median nerve and the soleus H-reflex latency. *J Neurol Neurosurg Psychiatry*. 1987;50:447–452.

MUSCULOCUTANEOUS MOTOR NERVE TO THE BICEPS BRACHII

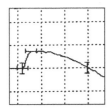 Typical waveform appearance

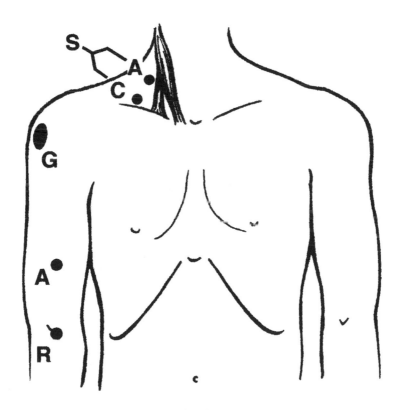

Electrode Placement

Position: This study is performed in the seated position.

Active electrode (A): Placement is just distal to the midportion of the biceps brachii muscle.

Reference electrode (R): Placement is proximal to the antecubital fossa in the region of the junction of the muscle fibers and the biceps tendon.

Ground electrode (G): Placement is on the acromion.

Stimulation point (S): Erb's point—the cathode is placed slightly above the upper margin of the clavicle lateral to the clavicular head of the sternocleidomastoid muscle. The anode is superomedial.

Machine settings: Sensitivity—5 mV/division, Low frequency filter—2 to 3 Hz, High frequency filter—10 kHz, Sweep speed—2 msec/division.

Nerve fibers tested: C5 and C6 nerve roots, through the upper trunk, anterior division, and lateral cord of the brachial plexus.

Reference values (1) (100 subjects) (temperature greater than or equal to 32°C):

Onset latency (msec)

Height in cm (in)	Mean	SD	Range	Upper Reference Value
<160 (5'3")	4.5	0.4	3.8–5.3	5.3
160–170 (5'3"–5'7")	4.7	0.4	3.9–5.6	5.6
>170 (5'7")	5.1	0.4	4.2–6.2	5.8
All subjects	4.8	0.5	3.8–6.2	5.6

Amplitude (mV)

Sex	Mean	SD	Range	Lower Reference Value
Male	10.1	3.3	3.8–21.1	4.0
Female	7.4	2.5	3.8–15.0	3.8
All subjects	8.7	3.2	3.8–21.1	4.0

Area of negative phase (mVms)

Sex	Mean	SD	Range	Lower Reference Value
Male	85.5	21.8	38.4–124.8	47.8
Female	61.6	18.2	26.1–97.3	34.5
All subjects	73.8	23.3	26.1–124.8	36.0

Duration of negative phase (msec)

Mean	SD	Range	Upper Reference Value
13.5	2.2	2.5–17.3	16.8

Acceptable Differences

The upper limit of normal increase in latency from one side to the other is 0.4 msec.

The upper limit of normal decrease in amplitude from one side to the other is 33%.

Notes

REFERENCE

1. Buschbacher RM, Weir SK, Bentley JR et al. Motor nerve conduction studies using surface electrode recording from supraspinatus, infraspinatus, deltoid, and biceps. *PM&R*. 2009;1:101–106.

ADDITIONAL READINGS

Gassel MM. A test of nerve conduction to muscles of the shoulder girdle as an aid in the diagnosis of proximal neurogenic and muscular disease. *J Neurol Neurosurg Psychiatry*. 1964;27:200–205.

Kraft GH. Axillary, musculocutaneous and suprascapular nerve latency studies. *Arch Phys Med Rehabil*. 1972;53:383–387.

Trojaborg W. Motor and sensory conduction in the musculocutaneous nerve. *J Neurol Neurosurg Psychiatry*. 1976;39(9):890–899.

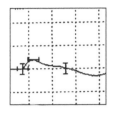

Typical waveform
appearance

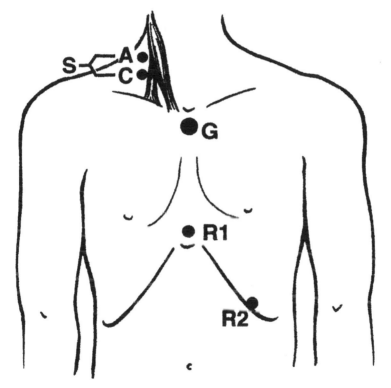

Electrode Placement

46

Position: This study is performed in the supine position, with the neck slightly neutral or extended (1).

Recording electrodes (R): In the cited study, self-adhesive 2.5 cm × 2.5 cm surface electrodes were used. One electrode (R1) is placed 5 cm superior to the tip of the xiphoid process. The other electrode (R2) is placed 16 cm distally along the lower costal margin (usually at the 7th intercostal space) (2).

Ground electrode (G): Placement is over the upper chest (3).

Stimulation point (S): Stimulation is applied at the posterior border of the sternocleidomastoid muscle in the supraclavicular fossa, with the cathode (C) approximately 3 cm superior to the clavicle. The anode (A) is superior to the cathode. In the cited study, two supramaximal responses were obtained and the results averaged (2).

Machine settings: Low frequency filter—5 Hz, High frequency filter—5 kHz.

Nerve fibers tested: C3, C4, and C5 nerve roots, and phrenic nerve.

Reference values (2) (25 subjects) (temperature not reported):

Onset latency (msec)

Mean	SD	Range	Suggested Reference Value
6.54	0.77	5.5–8.4	<8.1

Amplitude (μV)

Mean	SD	Range	Suggested Reference Value
660	201	301–1198	>300

Area (mVms)

Mean	SD	Range	Suggested Reference Value
7.28	2.09	4.0–12.8	>4.0

Duration from onset to return to baseline (msec)

Mean	SD	Range	Suggested Reference Value
19.4	2.7	13.4–24.1	<25

Acceptable Differences

Mean side-to-side difference for latency is 0.34 ± 0.27 msec with a range of 0 to 1.2 msec. The upper limit of normal difference, based on mean + 2 SD, is 0.88 msec.

Mean side-to-side difference for amplitude is 109 ± 94 μV with a range of 0 to 360 μV. The upper limit of normal difference, based on mean + 2 SD, is 39.5%.

Mean side-to-side difference for area is 1.41 ± 1.26 mVms with a range of 0.02 to 5.04 mVms. The upper limit of normal difference, based on mean + 2 SD, is 46.3%.

Mean side-to-side difference for duration is 2.26 ± 1.69 msec with a range of 0.15 to 6.2 msec. The upper limit of normal difference, based on mean + 2 SD, is 5.6 msec.

Helpful Hints

- Increasing age is associated with increasing latency. This may need to be taken into account when studying older subjects. A larger chest circumference is associated with increased amplitude (2).

- EKG artifact may occasionally be recorded as a prolonged (>50 msec duration), large amplitude response. The stimulus should be repeated until a valid response is obtained (1,2).

- Improper stimulus location may inadvertently activate the brachial plexus. This results in a volume conducted potential being recorded. The latency is shorter and there is an initial positive phase of the waveform. Brachial plexus stimulation may cause arm movement, arm paresthesias, and a short-latency, low-amplitude, initially positive response being recorded (1,2). Simultaneous recording over the deltoid (in a 2nd channel) can detect this.

- Deep breathing should be avoided during the testing. Quiet breathing should not interfere with the results (1).

- Because of amplitude variability, it may be helpful to repeat the study several times to obtain the two highest amplitudes; these should be relatively consistent.

- Needle stimulation and more anterior surface stimulation just medial and superior to the clavicular insertion of the sternocleidomastoid muscle may also be performed (4,5). Needle recording electrodes can also be used to improve amplitude and waveform consistency. We recommend the utilization of ultrasound guidance for placement of the needle.

- Visualization of the diaphragmatic twitch with diaphragm ultrasound or fluoroscopy when performing the nerve conduction study will help to confirm diaphragm contraction (6).

- Side-to-side difference in latency with needle stimulation has been described as 0.08 ± 0.42 msec (4).

Notes

_____

_____

_____

_____

_____

REFERENCES

1. Bolton CF. AAEM minimonograph #40: clinical neurophysiology of the respiratory system. *Muscle Nerve*. 1993;16:809–818.
2. Chen R, Collins S, Remtulla H, et al. Phrenic nerve conduction study in normal subjects. *Muscle Nerve*. 1995;18:330–335.
3. Markand ON, Kincaid JC, Pourmand RA, et al. Electrophysiologic evaluation of diaphragm by transcutaneous phrenic nerve stimulation. *Neurology*. 1984;34:604–614.
4. MacLean IC, Mattioni TA. Phrenic nerve conduction studies: a new technique and its application in quadriplegic patients. *Arch Phys Med Rehabil*. 1981;62:70–73.
5. Ma DM, Liveson JA. *Nerve Conduction Handbook*. Philadelphia, PA: FA Davis; 1983.
6. Johnson NE, Utz M, Patrick E, et al. Visualization of the diaphragm muscle with ultrasound improves diagnostic accuracy of phrenic nerve conduction studies. *Muscle Nerve*. 2014;49(5):669–675.

ADDITIONAL READINGS/ALTERNATE TECHNIQUES

Demoule A, Morelot-Panzini C, Prodanovic H, et al. Identification of prolonged phrenic nerve conduction time in the ICU: magnetic versus electrical stimulation. *Intensive Care Med*. 2011;37(12):1962–1968.

Russell RI, Helps BA, Elliot MJ, Helms PJ. Phrenic nerve stimulation at the bedside in children: equipment and validation. *Eur Respir J*. 1993;6:1332–1335.

Swenson MR, Rubenstein RS. Phrenic nerve conduction studies. *Muscle Nerve*. 1992;15:597–603.

RADIAL NERVE

RADIAL MOTOR NERVE TO THE EXTENSOR CARPI ULNARIS AND BRACHIORADIALIS

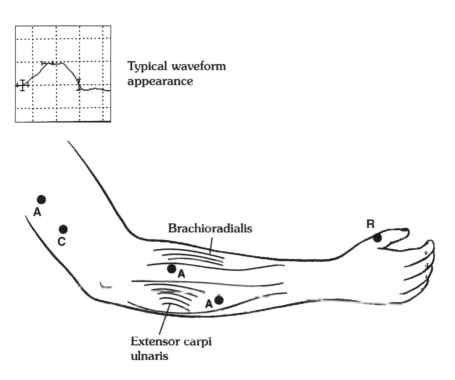

Typical waveform appearance

Brachioradialis

Extensor carpi ulnaris

Electrode Placement

Position: This study is performed in the supine position.

Active electrode (A): For the brachioradialis, placement is on the belly of the muscle, 3 cm distal to the elbow. For the extensor carpi ulnaris, placement is at the mid-forearm (equal distance between the lateral epicondyle and the ulnar styloid process), close to the "ulnar crease."

Reference electrode (R): Placement is on the thumb.

Stimulation: The cathode **(C)** is a monopolar needle electrode inserted 5 to 6 cm proximal to the lateral epicondyle on the lateral upper arm. This is ideally performed under ultrasound guidance. The anode **(A)** is a subcutaneous needle electrode located 2 cm proximally.

Machine settings: Sensitivity—2 to 5 mV/division, Sweep speed—3 msec/division, Low frequency filter—2 to 3 Hz, High frequency filter—10 kHz.

Nerve fibers tested: Extensor carpi ulnaris: C6, C7, and C8 nerve roots, through the upper, middle, and lower trunks, posterior divisions, and posterior cord of the brachial plexus, then through the radial nerve and the posterior interosseous branch of the radial nerve. Brachioradialis: C5 and C6 nerve roots, through the upper trunk, posterior division, posterior cord of the brachial plexus, and then radial nerve.

Reference values (1) (40 subjects—data for both sides combined) (skin temperature over palm and forearm greater than 31°C):

Onset latency (msec)

Brachioradialis

	Mean	SD	Range	Upper Reference Value
	2.66	0.32	1.8–3.5	3.3

Extensor carpi ulnaris

	Mean	SD	Range	Upper Reference Value
	4.00	0.35	3.1–5.2	4.2

Acceptable Differences

The upper limit of normal difference in latency between the extensor carpi ulnaris versus the brachioradialis is 1.8 msec (mean 1.34 ± 0.23, range 0.8–2.0).

The upper limit of normal side-to-side difference in latency is 0.4 msec (mean 0.19 ± 0.06, range 0.0–0.4).

Helpful Hints

- The nerve branch to the brachioradialis does not pass through the "radial tunnel," whereas the branch to the extensor carpi ulnaris does.

- The author states that needle stimulation is preferable to surface stimulation because surface stimulation at this point often requires painful high-intensity stimulation and often causes electrical artifacts. Needle stimulation also localizes the stimulation site more precisely.

Notes

REFERENCE

1. Seror P. Posterior interosseous nerve conduction: a new method of evaluation. *Am J Phys Med Rehabil*. 1996;75:35–39.

ADDITIONAL READING

Mondelli M, Morana P, Ballerini M, et al. Mononeuropathies of the radial nerve: clinical and neurographic findings in 91 consecutive cases. *J Electromyogr Kinesiol*. 2005;15(4):377–383.

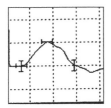

Typical waveform
appearance

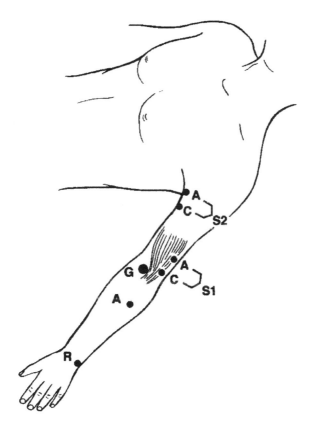

Electrode Placement

Position: This study is performed in the supine position.

Active electrode (A): Placement is 8 cm distal to stimulation point 1 over the extensor digitorum. This site is localized in the reference (1) by grasping the radius and ulna of the subject's pronated forearm with a line between the thumb and middle finger and the junction of the upper third and middle third of the forearm. The index finger is placed halfway between these two points to identify the extensor digitorum. Confirmation is obtained by asking the patient to extend the MCP joints.

Reference electrode (R): Placement is over the ulnar styloid process.

Ground electrode (G): Placement is between the stimulating and recording electrodes.

Stimulation point 1 (S1): The cathode (C) is placed in the antecubital fossa just lateral to the biceps tendon as the tendon crosses the flexor crease. The anode (A) is proximal. The arm is supported and abducted 40 to 45 degrees.

Stimulation point 2 (S2): The cathode (C) is placed in the axilla between the coracobrachialis and the long head of the triceps. The anode (A) is proximal.

Machine settings: Sensitivity—5 mV/division, Low frequency filter—5 Hz, High frequency filter—10 kHz, Sweep speed—5 msec/division.

Nerve fibers tested: C7 and C8 nerve roots, through the middle and lower trunks, posterior divisions, and posterior cord of the brachial plexus, then through the radial nerve and posterior interosseous branch of the radial nerve.

Reference values For the right side (left side results were similar) (1) (30 subjects) (skin temperature over the forearm greater than or equal to 34°C) (reference values derived by using mean ± 2 SD):

Onset latency (msec)

Mean	SD	Upper Reference Value
2.6	0.44	3.5

Amplitude (mV)

Mean	SD	Lower Reference Value
11.31	3.5	4.3

Nerve conduction velocity between S1 and S2 (m/sec)—the distance is measured from the axilla, measure posteriorly, to the elbow stimulation site [caliper measurement should give a similar distance measurement (2)].

Mean	SD	Lower Reference Value
68	7.0	54

Helpful Hints

- With proximal stimulation there can be a problem of recording volume conducted potentials from other muscles. Therefore, only the minimal stimulus intensity necessary to produce a waveform similar in appearance to that on distal stimulation is recommended.

- Rotation of the anode may be necessary to obtain an optimal recording.

- Calculation of reference values using mean ± 2 SD may produce misleading results when distributions are skewed; thus use the previous values with caution.

Notes

REFERENCES

1. Young AW, Redmond MD, Hemler DE, Belandres PV. Radial motor nerve conduction studies. *Arch Phys Med Rehabil.* 1990;71:399–402.
2. Kalantri A, Visser BD, Dumitru D, Grant AE. Axilla to elbow radial nerve conduction. *Muscle Nerve.* 1988;11:133–135.

ADDITIONAL READINGS/ALTERNATE TECHNIQUES

Humphries R, Currier DP. Variables in recording motor conduction of the radial nerve. *Phys Ther.* 1976;56(7):809–814.
Kupfer DM, Bronson J, Lee GW, et al. Differential latency testing: a more sensitive test for radial tunnel syndrome. *J Hand Surg.* 1998;23A:859–864.

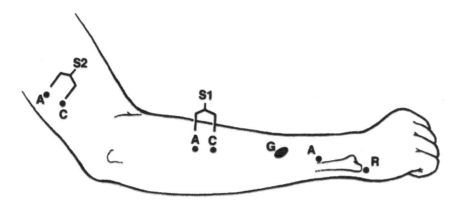

Electrode Placement

Position: This study is performed in the supine position. For surface recording, the elbow is extended and the forearm fully pronated.

Active electrode (A): Placement is 4 cm proximal to the ulnar styloid, over the motor point of the extensor indicis.

Reference electrode (R): Placement is over the ulnar styloid.

Ground electrode (G): Placement over the dorsal forearm.

Stimulation point 1 (S1): The cathode is placed 8 cm proximal to the active electrode. The anode is proximal.

Stimulation point 2 (S2): The cathode is placed 8 to 10 cm proximal to the lateral epicondyle, over the radial groove. The anode is proximal.

F-wave stimulation: Electrode setup as noted previously (A, R, G). The antecubital region is stimulated just lateral to the biceps tendon, with the cathode proximal.

Machine settings: Sensitivity—2 mV/division, Low frequency filter—10 Hz, High frequency filter—10 kHz, Sweep speed—2 msec/division.

Nerve fibers tested: C7 and C8 nerve roots, through the middle and lower trunks, posterior divisions, and posterior cord of the brachial plexus, then through the radial nerve and the posterior interosseous branch of the radial nerve.

Reference values (1) (skin temperature over the ventral forearm at least 33°C):

Onset latency (msec—25 subjects)

Mean	SD
2.1	0.2

Amplitude (mV—25 subjects)

Mean	SD	Range
4.5	1.8	1.7–11.1

Nerve conduction velocity (m/sec—25 subjects)

Mean	SD	Range
71.7	4.7	60.2–79.2

F-wave latencies (msec—23 subjects)

Mean	SD	Range
19.8	3.7	16.2–24.1

Notes

RADIAL MOTOR NERVE TO THE EXTENSOR INDICIS: NEEDLE RECORDING

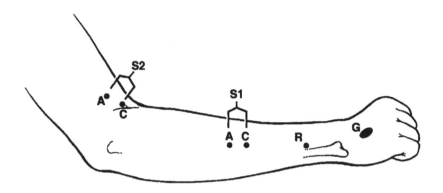

Electrode Placement

Position: This study is performed in the supine position.

Recording electrodes (R): A concentric needle electrode is placed (preferably using ultrasound guidance) into the extensor indicis on the dorsal forearm (2). The muscle is slightly radial to the ulna and extensor carpi ulnaris tendon, approximately 4 cm proximal to the ulnar styloid process, and approximately one half-inch deep. Monopolar needle electrode recording has also been described with a surface reference electrode placed on the 5th digit (3,4).

Ground electrode (G): Placement is over the dorsum of the hand or between the stimulating and recording electrodes.

Stimulation point 1 (S1): The cathode (C) is placed 3 to 4 cm proximal to the needle insertion site between the extensor carpi ulnaris and the extensor digiti minimi. The anode (A) is proximal (4).

Stimulation point (S2): The cathode (C) is placed 5 to 6 cm proximal to the lateral epicondyle in the groove between the brachialis and brachioradialis muscles. The anode (A) is proximal.

Stimulation point 3 (S3): The stimulating electrodes are placed at Erb's point.

Machine settings: Standard motor settings are used.

Reference values:

Onset latency over 2.8 to 6.6 cm distance (msec) (29 subjects, monopolar needle recording) (3)

Mean	SD	Range
1.69	0.29	1.0–2.0

Nerve conduction velocity (the distal segment is measured with a tape measure, the proximal segment with obstetric calipers; arm abducted 10 degrees, elbow flexed 10–15 degrees, forearm pronated, head rotated away from side being tested)

S1–S2 nerve conduction velocity (m/sec) (49 subjects) (2)

Mean	SD	Range
61.6	5.9	48–75

S2–S3 nerve conduction velocity (m/sec) (49 subjects) (2)

Mean	SD	Range
72.0	6.3	56–93

Acceptable Difference

If the proximal velocity is less than 60 m/sec or if the distal velocity is more than 6 m/sec faster than the proximal velocity, an abnormality of conduction in the proximal segment may be suspected (2).

Helpful Hints

- Surface or needle recording has been described. It is important that the shape of the waveform be similar with proximal and distal stimulation (3,4).

- The site of needle insertion can usually be localized by first having the subject flex and extend the index finger while palpating the muscle. The needle is inserted and proper placement is confirmed by free-run electromyography or ultrasound.

- The preceding nerve conduction velocity results were obtained with a concentric needle recording, but the same author also described monopolar needle recording from the same muscle (4). He found that this did not consistently provide a negative takeoff with Erb's point stimulation. It seems reasonable to substitute a monopolar needle (with ultrasound guidance) as long as proper care is given to recording an accurate onset of the waveform.

- An armboard may help to stabilize the forearm and prevent needle movement (2).

- A needle stimulation technique has also been described and recommended as more accurate than surface stimulation (5,6). We recommend ultrasound guidance for proper needle placement.

- Axillary stimulation can also be performed. In a study that utilized needle stimulation and recording, the distal latency was 2.4 ± 0.5 msec, axilla to above elbow nerve conduction velocity was 69 ± 5.6 m/sec, and above elbow to forearm nerve conduction velocity was 62 ± 5.1 m/sec (5).

Notes _____

_____

_____

_____

_____

_____

_____

_____

_____

_____

_____

REFERENCES

1. Date ES, Teraoka JK, Chan J, Kingery WS. Effects of elbow flexion on radial nerve motor conduction velocity. *Electromyogr Clin Neurophysiol*. 2002;42:51–56.
2. Jebsen RH. Motor conduction velocity in proximal and distal segments of the radial nerve. *Arch Phys Med Rehabil*. 1966;47:597–602.
3. Ma DM, Liveson JA. *Nerve Conduction Handbook*. Philadelphia, PA: FA Davis; 1983.
4. Jebsen RH. Motor conduction velocity of distal radial nerve. *Arch Phys Med Rehabil*. 1966;47:12–16.
5. Trojaborg W, Sindrup EH. Motor and sensory conduction in different segments of the radial nerve in normal subjects. *J Neurol Neurosurg Psychiatry*. 1969;32:354–359.
6. Falck B, Hurme M. Conduction velocity of the posterior interosseous nerve across the arcade of Frohse. *Electromyogr Clin Neurophysiol*. 1983;23:567–576.

SUPRASCAPULAR MOTOR NERVE TO THE SUPRASPINATUS AND INFRASPINATUS

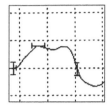

Typical waveform
appearance

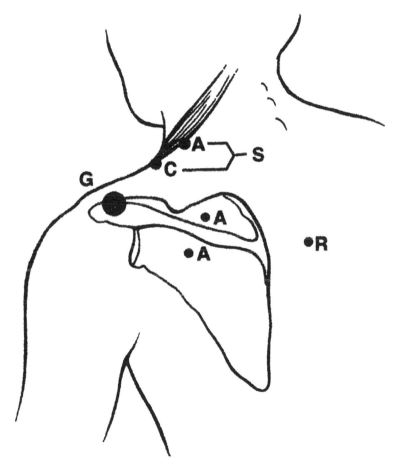

Electrode Placement

Position: This study is performed in the seated position.

Active electrode (A): For the supraspinatus, placement is 2 cm medial to the midpoint of the spine of the scapula. For the infraspinatus, placement is 2 cm inferior to the midpoint of the spine of the scapula.

Reference electrode (R): Placement is on the midline thoracic spine at the same level.

Ground electrode (G): Placement is on the acromion.

Stimulation point (S): Erb's point—the cathode (C) is placed slightly above the upper margin of the clavicle lateral to the clavicular head of the sternocleidomastoid muscle. The anode (A) is superomedial.

Machine settings: Sensitivity—5 mV/division, Low frequency filter—2 to 3 Hz, High frequency filter—10 kHz, Sweep speed—2 msec/division.

Nerve fibers tested: C5 and C6 nerve roots, through the upper trunk of the brachial plexus and suprascapular nerve.

Reference values (1) (100 subjects) (temperature greater than or equal to 32°C):

Onset latency (msec)

Supraspinatus

Height in cm (in)	Mean	SD	Range	Upper Reference Value
≤170 (5'7")	3.1	0.4	2.0–4.1	3.7
>170 (5'7")	3.4	0.6	2.3–5.2	4.6
All subjects	3.2	0.5	2.0–5.2	4.3

Infraspinatus

Height in cm (in)	Mean	SD	Range	Upper Reference Value
≤170 (5'7")	3.4	0.4	2.6–4.3	4.1
>170 (5'7")	3.9	0.7	2.7–6.1	5.4
All subjects	3.6	0.6	2.6–6.1	4.8

Amplitude (mV)

Supraspinatus

Mean	SD	Range	Lower Reference Value
3.7	2.3	1.2–12.6	1.6

Infraspinatus

Sex	Mean	SD	Range	Lower Reference Value
Male	3.5	1.5	1.4–7.8	1.5
Female	4.1	1.7	1.4–8.6	1.4
All subjects	3.8	1.6	1.4–8.6	1.5

Area of negative phase (mVms)

Supraspinatus

Mean	SD	Range	Lower Reference Value
14.7	11.5	3.5–53.0	4.0

Infraspinatus

Mean	SD	Range	Lower Reference Value
14.0	5.7	3.5–30.3	5.0

Duration of negative phase (msec)

Supraspinatus

Mean	SD	Range	Upper Reference Value
6.7	2.8	2.9–14.2	13.5

Infraspinatus

Height in cm (in)	Mean	SD	Range	Upper Reference Value
≤160 (5′7″)	5.1	1.6	2.8–9.1	9.1
>160 (5′7″)	6.3	2.3	2.3–13.9	10.7
All subjects	5.9	2.2	2.3–13.9	10.1

Acceptable Differences

The upper limit of normal increase in supraspinatus latency from one side to the other is 0.7 msec.

The upper limit of normal increase in infraspinatus latency from one side to the other is 0.4 msec.

The upper limit of normal decrease in supraspinatus amplitude from one side to the other is 48%.

The upper limit of normal decrease in infraspinatus amplitude from one side to the other is 48%.

The upper limit of normal increase in latency between supraspinatus and infraspinatus recording on the same side is 1.6 msec.

Notes _____

_____

_____

_____

_____

_____

_____

_____

_____

_____

REFERENCE

1. Buschbacher RM, Weir SK, Bentley JR et al. Motor nerve conduction studies using surface electrode recording from supraspinatus, infraspinatus, deltoid, and biceps. *PM&R*. 2009;1:101–106.

ADDITIONAL READINGS

Casazza BS, Young JL, Press JP, Heinemann AW. Suprascapular nerve conduction: a comparative analysis in normal subjects. *Electromyogr Clin Neurophysiol*. 1998;38:153–160.

Clark JD, King RB, Ashman E. Detection of suprascapular nerve lesions using surface recording electrodes. Presented at: The AAEM Annual Meeting; September 20, 1997.

Edgar TS, Lotz BP. A nerve conduction technique for the evaluation of suprascapular neuropathies. Presented at: The AAEM Annual Meeting; October 16, 1998; Orlando, FL.

Ma DM, Liveson JA. *Nerve Conduction Handbook*. Philadelphia, PA: FA Davis; 1983.

THORACODORSAL MOTOR NERVE TO THE LATISSIMUS DORSI

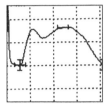

Typical waveform
appearance

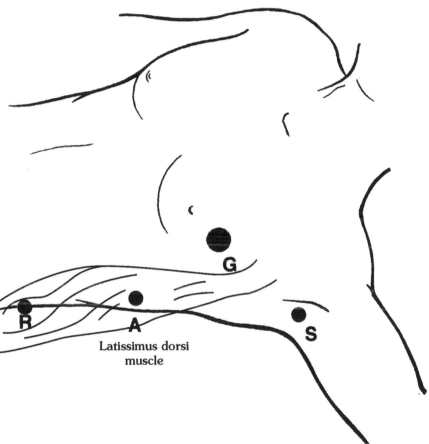

Latissimus dorsi
muscle

Electrode Placement

Position: This study is performed in the supine position.

Active electrode (A): Placement is on the posterior axillary line at the level of the inferior pole of the scapula.

Reference electrode (R): Placement is on the ipsilateral flank.

Ground electrode (G): Placement is on the ipsilateral lateral chest wall.

Stimulation point (S): The cathode is placed in the axilla with the anode proximal. The subject is supine, with the shoulder abducted to 90 degrees.

Machine settings: Sensitivity—2 mV/division, Low frequency filter—2 Hz, High frequency filter—10 kHz, Sweep speed—1 msec/division, Pulse duration—0.2 msec.

Nerve fibers tested: C6, C7, and C8 nerve roots, through the upper, middle, and lower trunks, posterior divisions, posterior cord of the brachial plexus, and thoracodorsal nerve.

Reference values (1) (30 subjects—right side data) (temperature not reported):

Onset latency (msec)

Mean	SD	Range	Upper Reference Value
1.9	0.4	1.2–2.7	2.7

Amplitude (mV)

Mean	SD	Range
4.1	1.8	1.4–10.2

Acceptable Difference

The upper limit of normal decrease in amplitude from one side to the other is 50%.

Helpful Hints

- The latissimus dorsi can be localized by asking the subject to depress and internally rotate the shoulder.

- The distance between the stimulation point and the active electrode ranged from 5 to 12 cm, measured with a tape measure with the shoulder abducted 90 degrees.

- In obese subjects it may be helpful to press the stimulator deeper into the axilla toward the lateral margin of the scapula to obtain a response.

- In the cited study, Erb's point stimulation was performed to calculate a conduction velocity across the axillary segment. This measure was not deemed to be reliable.

Notes _____

REFERENCE

1. Wu PBJ, Robinson T, Kingery WS, Date ES. Thoracodorsal nerve conduction study. *Am J Phys Med Rehabil.* 1998;77:296–298.

ADDITIONAL READING/ALTERNATE TECHNIQUE

Lo Monaco M, Di Pasqua PG, Tonali P. Conduction studies along the accessory, long thoracic, dorsal scapular, and thoracodorsal nerves. *Acta Neurol Scand.* 1983;68:171–176.

ULNAR NERVE

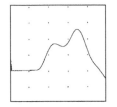

Typical waveform
appearance

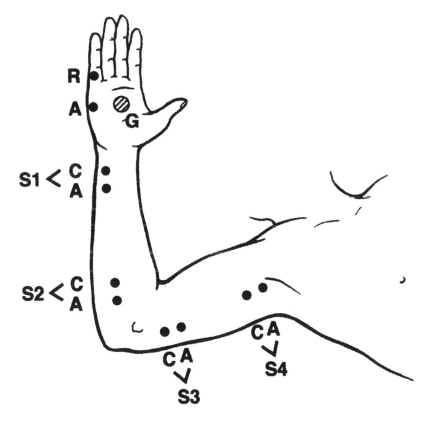

Electrode Placement

74

Position: For this study the arm is positioned in a 45-degree abducted and externally rotated posture. The elbow is flexed to 90 degrees (right angle) and the forearm is in neutral position (thumb pointing toward the ear).

Active electrode (A): Placement is on the ulnar surface of the hypothenar eminence, halfway between the level of the pisiform bone and the 5th MCP joint.

Reference electrode (R): Placement is slightly distal to the 5th MCP joint.

Ground electrode (G): Placement is on the dorsum of the hand. If stimulus artifact interferes with the recording, the ground may be placed near the active electrode, between this electrode and the cathode.

Stimulation point 1 (S1): The cathode (C) is placed 8 cm proximal to the active electrode, in a line measured slightly radial to the tendon of the flexor carpi ulnaris. The anode (A) is proximal.

Stimulation point 2 (S2): The cathode (C) is placed approximately 4 cm distal to the medial epicondyle. The anode (A) is proximal.

Stimulation point 3 (S3): The cathode (C) is placed approximately 10 cm proximal to stimulation point 2, measured in a curve behind the medial epicondyle to a point slightly volar to the triceps. The anode (A) is proximal.

Stimulation point 4 (S4): The cathode (C) is placed in the axilla approximately 10 cm proximal to stimulation point 3. The anode (A) is proximal.

F-wave stimulation: The cathode (C) is positioned as for stimulation point 1, but with the anode distal.

Machine settings: Sensitivity—5 mV/division, Low frequency filter—2 to 3 Hz, High frequency filter—10 kHz, Sweep speed—2 msec/division.

Nerve fibers tested: C8 and T1 nerve roots, through the lower trunk, anterior division, medial cord of the brachial plexus, and ulnar nerve.

Reference values (1) (248 subjects) (skin temperature over the dorsum of the hand greater than or equal to 32°C):

Onset latency (msec)

Mean	SD	Range	Upper Reference Value
3.0	0.3	2.3–4.4	3.7

Amplitude (mV)

Mean	SD	Range	Lower Reference Value
11.6	2.1	6.3–18.0	7.9

Area of negative phase (mVms)

Mean	SD	Range	Lower Reference Value
35.9	7.1	19.9–63.2	23.9

Duration of negative phase (msec)

Mean	SD	Range	Upper Reference Value
6.0	0.9	3.8–8.4	7.7

Nerve conduction velocity (m/sec)

	Mean	SD	Range	Lower Reference Value
S1–S2	61	5	49–74	52
S2–S3	61	9	35–83	43
S3–S4	61	7	44–87	50

F-wave latencies (msec) (2) (193 subjects)—shortest of 10 stimuli

	Age Range 19–49			
Height in cm (in)	Mean	SD	Range	Upper Reference Value
<160 (5'3")	23.5	1.3	20.3–26.3	26.1
160–179 (5'3"–5'10")	26.2	2.0	22.4–31.1	30.2
≥180 (5'11")	29.2	1.8	26.2–32.9	32.8

	Age Range 50 79			
Height in cm (in)	Mean	SD	Range	Upper Reference Value
<160 (5'3")	25.0	1.9	22.9–28.4	28.8
160–179 (5'3"–5'10")	28.1	1.4	26.3–30.8	30.9
≥180 (5'11")	30.4	1.7	28.3–32.4	33.8
All subjects	26.5	2.5	20.3–32.9	31.5

Acceptable Differences

The upper limit of normal increase in latency from one side to the other is 0.6 msec.

The upper limit of normal decrease in amplitude from one side to the other is 25%.

The upper limit of normal decrease in nerve conduction velocity from the S1–S2 to S2–S3 segment is 15 m/sec.

The upper limit of normal decrease in S1 to S2 nerve conduction velocity from one side to the other is 9 m/sec.

The upper limit of normal decrease in S2 to S3 nerve conduction velocity from one side to the other is 17 m/sec.

The upper limit of normal decrease in S3 to S4 nerve conduction velocity from one side to the other is 16 m/sec.

The upper limit of normal decrease in amplitude from S1 to S2 stimulation is 35%.

The upper limit of normal decrease in amplitude from S2 to S3 stimulation is 16%.

The upper limit of normal decrease in amplitude from S3 to S4 stimulation is 21%.

The upper limit of normal side to side difference in the shortest F-wave latency is 2.5 msec.

The upper limit of normal difference between median (APB) and ulnar (ADM) motor latency in the same limb is 1.4 msec (ages 19–49), 1.7 msec (ages 50–79), and 1.5 msec (all subjects) in cases where the median has the longer latency; it is 0.0 msec (ages 19–49), –0.3 msec (ages 50–79), and 0.0 msec (all subjects) in cases where the ulnar latency is longer (3).

Helpful Hints

- More proximal stimulation can also be performed at Erb's point in the supraclavicular fossa. This can allow determination of waveform changes across a more proximal segment of the nerve and calculation of more proximal nerve conduction velocity. When calculating the conduction velocity of the Erb's point-to-axilla segment, obstetric calipers are used to measure the distance.

- Assessment of C8 nerve root can be performed by needle stimulation and recording over the hypothenar eminence. Livingstone et al. (4) describe the best position for upper extremity measurement of mid-humerus-cervical spine distance as at 60 degrees of shoulder abduction, 45 degrees of internal rotation, and at the distance of 35 cm, measured by caliper. Using this position and distance the following normal values were obtained ($n = 20$):

1. Mid-humerus F-wave minimal latencies were 21.8 ± 1.2 msec, and conduction velocity was 59.7 ± 2.4 m/sec.

2. C8 root stimulation and latency difference to the mid-humerus was 4.9 ± 0.2 msec with a velocity of 71.4 ± 2.2 m/sec, (4).

- Anomalous innervation due to a Martin–Gruber (median to ulnar) anastomosis in the forearm is common. It may result in a smaller ulnar compound motor action potential amplitude at the elbow than the wrist, and can simulate conduction block in the forearm. If suspected, it can be investigated by stimulating the median nerve in the elbow, while recording from ADM. For more information please refer to the median nerve section.

- The ulnar nerve motor response to the abductor digiti minimi may be normal in Guyon's canal entrapment neuropathy at the wrist, as this muscle is usually innervated by the superficial palmar branch of the ulnar nerve. If such a compression is suspected, the motor responses to the first dorsal interosseous or palmar interosseous muscles should be studied.

- Recording a response with S2 stimulation may at times be difficult, especially in obese or muscular individuals. It may be necessary to move the cathode around to find the optimal stimulation site, including moving it proximally. Increased stimulus intensity or duration or needle stimulation may occasionally be needed. When moving from the S2 to S3 site, the intensity should be lowered before stimulation because the nerve is much easier to stimulate at this site.

- Occasionally an optimal amplitude cannot be obtained at S2 stimulation. This may give the false impression of a conduction block in the forearm. If S3 stimulation provides a normal amplitude, such a conduction block is not present and one should go back to S2 stimulation to see if a larger response can be obtained.

- An "inching technique" called short segment incremental stimulation (SSIS) can be performed to localize the site of an ulnar neuropathy at the elbow (UNE). First the nerve's course is mapped out with subthreshold stimuli by moving the stimulator perpendicular to the nerve's course until the maximal M-wave amplitude for a given subthreshold intensity is obtained. This point is marked with a dot. This process is repeated along the length of the nerve, and the dots are joined to outline the course of the nerve. Then supramaximal stimulation is performed in 1-cm increments along the length of the nerve, taking care not to apply excessively supramaximal stimulation. The upper limit of normal segmental latency change is 0.4 msec. Abrupt changes in waveform shape or amplitude may be signs of local conduction block (5). The upper limit of normal segmental latency change recorded in 2-cm increments (elbow fixed at 90 degrees of flexion) is 0.7 msec. The midpoint is determined by drawing a line between the medial epicondyle and the olecranon. Focal demyelination is more likely when focal slowing and conduction block are seen at the same site. The upper limit of normal latency change (msec) and amplitude change (%) follow (6).

	Latency	Amplitude
4 cm to 2 cm above elbow	0.63	13
2 cm above elbow to midpoint	0.84	12
Midpoint to 2 cm below elbow	0.74	10
2 cm to 4 cm below elbow	0.43	20

- UNE may be due to compression at any of three sites: the retroepicondylar groove, the humeroulnar aponeurotic arcade, and the deep forearm aponeurosis at the point of exit from under the flexor carpi ulnaris (Pridgeon's point). If possible, it is advisable to try to localize an ulnar neuropathy to one or more of these sites through incremental stimulation (5).

- The terms *cubital tunnel syndrome* and *tardy ulnar palsy* are poorly defined, are often if not usually misapplied, and should be discarded. The term *ulnar neuropathy at the elbow* (UNE) should be used instead.

- The Riche-Cannieu anastomosis (sometimes referred to as the "All Ulnar Hand") most likely results from palmar communication between ulnar and median branches (Riche-Cannieu anastomoses). There was no evidence of anomalous communication in the forearm. Digital sensory fibers were normally distributed in median and ulnar nerves (7–9).

Notes

REFERENCES

1. Buschbacher RM. Ulnar nerve motor conduction to the abductor digiti minimi. *Am J Phys Med Rehabil.* 1999;78:S9–S14.

2. Buschbacher RM. Ulnar nerve F-waves. *Am J Phys Med Rehabil.* 1999;78:S38–S42.

3. Grossart EA, Prahlow ND, Buschbacher RM. Acceptable differences in sensory and motor latencies between the median and ulnar nerves. *J Long Term Eff Med Implants.* 2006;16(5):395–400.

4. Livingstone EF, DeLisa JA, Halar EM. Electrodiagnostic values through the thoracic outlet using C8 root needle studies, F-wave, and cervical somatosensory evoked potentials. *Arch Phys Med Rehabil.* 1984;65(11):726–730.

5. Campbell WW, Pridgeon RM, Sahni KS. Short segment incremental studies in the evaluation of ulnar neuropathy at the elbow. *Muscle Nerve.* 1992;15:1050–1054.

6. Visser LH, Beekman R, Franssen H. Short-segment nerve conduction studies in ulnar neuropathy at the elbow. *Muscle Nerve.* 2005;31:331–338.

7. Brown JV, Landau ME. Sparing of the second lumbrical in a Riche-Cannieu anastomosis: the nearly all-ulnar hand. *J Clin Neuromuscul Dis.* 2013;14(4):184–187

8. Johnson EW. Comments on "Unilateral all Ulnar hand including sensory without forearm communication". *Am J Phys Med Rehabil.* 2004;83(12):936.

9. Dumitru D, Walsh NE, Weber CF. Electrophysiologic study of the Riche Cannieu Anomaly. *Electromyogr Clin Neurophysiol.* 1988;28(1):27–31.

ADDITIONAL READINGS

American Association of Electrodiagnostic Medicine, American Academy of Neurology, American Academy of Physical Medicine & Rehabilitation. Practice parameter for electrodiagnostic studies in ulnar neuropathy at the elbow: summary statement. *Muscle Nerve.* 1999;22:408–411.

Campbell WW. The value of inching techniques in the diagnosis of focal nerve lesions. *Muscle Nerve.* 1998;21:1154–1561.

Falco FJE, Hennessey WJ, Braddom RL, Goldberg G. Standardized nerve conduction studies in the upper limb of the healthy elderly. *Am J Phys Med Rehabil.* 1992;71:263–271.

Hennessey WJ, Falco FJE, Braddom RL. Median and ulnar nerve conduction studies: normative data for young adults. *Arch Phys Med Rehabil.* 1994;75:259–264.

Kanakamedala RV, Simons DG, Porter RW, Zucker RS. Ulnar nerve entrapment at the elbow localized by short segment stimulation. *Arch Phys Med Rehabil.* 1988;69:959–963.

Kincaid JC, Phillips LH, Daube JR. The evaluation of suspected ulnar neuropathy at the elbow: normal conduction study values. *Arch Neurol.* 1986;43:44–47.

Perez MC, Sosa A, Acevedo CEL. Nerve conduction velocities: normal values for median and ulnar nerves. *Bol Asoc Med P Rico.* 1986;78:191–196.

ULNAR MOTOR NERVE TO THE PALMAR INTEROSSEOUS (*SEE ALSO* MEDIAN MOTOR NERVE TO THE 2ND LUMBRICAL)

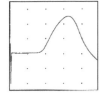

Typical waveform appearance

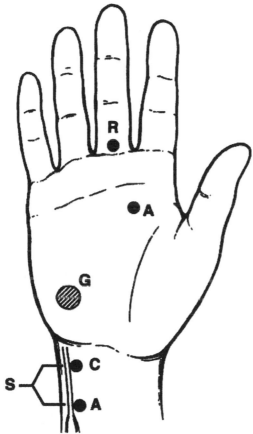

Electrode Placement

See also page 34 for the Median Motor Nerve to the 2nd Lumbrical.

Position: This study is performed in the supine position.

Active electrode (A): Placement is on the palm, slightly radial to the midpoint of the third metacarpal.

Reference electrode (R): Placement is slightly distal to the third MCP joint.

Ground electrode (G): Placement is on the dorsum of the hand.

Stimulation point (S): The cathode (C) is placed 10 cm proximal to the active electrode, slightly to the radial side of the tendon of the flexor carpi ulnaris. The anode (A) is proximal.

Machine settings: Sensitivity—5 mV/division, Low frequency filter—2 to 3 Hz, High frequency filter—10 kHz, Sweep speed—2 msec/division.

Nerve fibers tested: C8 and T1 nerve roots, through the lower trunk, anterior division, medial cord of the brachial plexus, and ulnar nerve.

Reference values (1) (196 subjects) (skin temperature over the dorsum of the hand greater than or equal to 32°C):

Onset latency (msec)

Mean	SD	Range	Upper Reference Value
3.1	0.3	2.6–4.4	4.0

Amplitude (mV)

Mean	SD	Range	Lower Reference Value
6.9	2.3	1.7–15.4	3.0

Area of negative phase (mVms)

Mean	SD	Range	Lower Reference Value
17.4	6.6	4.4–42.3	6.9

Duration of negative phase (msec)

Mean	SD	Range	Upper Reference Value
4.6	0.7	2.7–6.8	6.3

Acceptable Differences

The upper limit of normal increase in latency from one side to the other is 0.5 msec.

The upper limit of normal decrease in amplitude from one side to the other is 58%.

The upper limit of normal difference between 2nd lumbrical and interosseous latency in the same limb is 0.2 msec in cases where the interosseous has the longer latency; it is 1.2 msec in cases where the 2nd lumbrical latency is longer.

Helpful Hints

- Concomitant median and ulnar nerve stimulation must be avoided.

- The second lumbrical and interosseous muscles lie superimposed in this location. Stimulating the median nerve activates the lumbrical, whereas stimulating the ulnar nerve activates the interosseous muscle. Both nerve studies have approximately the same latencies and can thus be compared to detect slowing of one nerve or the other.

- Anomalous innervation is common and may result in no response being seen to stimulation of one of the involved nerves.

Notes

REFERENCE

1. Foley BS, Buschbacher RM. Establishing normal nerve conduction values; lumbrical and interosseous responses. *J Long Term Eff Med Implants.* 2006;16(5):359–368.

ADDITIONAL READINGS

Kothari MJ, Preston DC, Logigian EL. Lumbrical-interossei motor studies localize ulnar neuropathy at the wrist. *Muscle Nerve.* 1996;19:170–174.

Löscher WN, Auer-Grumbach M, Trinka E, et al. Comparison of second lumbrical and interosseous latencies with standard measures of median nerve function across the carpal tunnel: a prospective study of 450 hands. *J Neurol.* 2000;247:530–534.

Preston DC, Logigian EL. Lumbrical and interossei recording in carpal tunnel syndrome. *Muscle Nerve.* 1992;15:1253–1257.

ULNAR MOTOR NERVE TO THE 1ST DORSAL INTEROSSEOUS

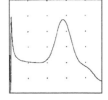

Typical waveform
appearance

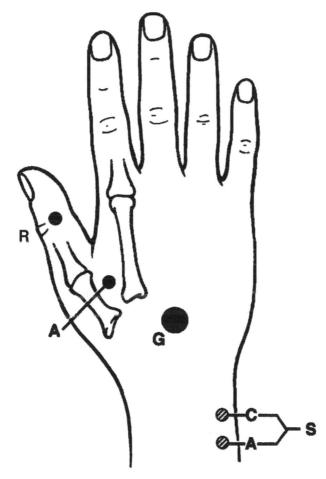

Electrode Placement

Position: This study is performed in the supine position.

Active electrode (A): Placement is on the dorsum of the first web space, in the center of the triangle formed by the first carpometacarpal joint, the first MCP joint, and the second MCP joint.

Reference electrode (R): Placement is slightly distal to the thumb IP joint.

Ground electrode (G): Placement is on the dorsum of the hand.

Stimulation point (S): The cathode (C) is placed at the S1 stimulation point for the ulnar motor nerve study to the abductor digiti minimi.

Machine settings: Sensitivity—5 mV/division, Low frequency filter—2 to 3 Hz, High frequency filter—10 kHz, Sweep speed—2 msec/division.

Nerve fibers tested: C8 and T1 nerve roots, through the lower trunk, anterior division, and medial cord of the brachial plexus and the deep palmar branch of the ulnar nerve.

Reference values (1) (100 subjects) (skin temperature over the dorsum of the hand greater than or equal to 32°C):

Onset latency (msec)

	Mean	SD	Range	Upper Reference Value
All subjects	3.4	0.3	2.8–4.5	4.0

Amplitude (mV)

Mean	SD	Range	Lower Reference Value
15.8	4.2	8.8–26.1	9.2

Acceptable Differences

The upper limit of normal increase in latency from one side to the other is 0.8 msec.

The upper limit of normal decrease in amplitude from one side to the other is 52%.

The upper limit of normal difference between first dorsal interosseous and abductor digiti minimi latency in the same limb is 1.3 msec.

Helpful Hints

- If information about more proximal ulnar nerve conduction velocity is desired, it should be obtained by studying the nerve to the abductor digiti minimi. Stimulation at the more proximal sites often activates both the median and the ulnar nerves, which causes volume conduction artifact to be recorded when studying the 1st dorsal interosseous muscle.

- Anomalous innervation of the 1st dorsal interosseous muscle is sometimes present. This is the muscle most commonly innervated by crossing fibers of the Martin–Gruber anastomosis.

- In 82% of subjects the amplitude to the 1st dorsal interosseous is greater than that recorded from the abductor digiti minimi.

Notes _____

_____

_____

_____

_____

REFERENCE

1. Buschbacher RM, Bayindir O, Malec J, Akyuz G. Ulnar motor study to first dorsal interosseous muscle: best reference electrode position and normative data. *Muscle Nerve*. 2015;52(2):231–233.

ADDITIONAL READINGS

Olney RK, Wilbourn AJ. Ulnar nerve conduction study of the first dorsal interosseous muscle. *Arch Phys Med Rehabil*. 1985;66:16–18.

Olney RK, Hanson M. AAEE case report #15: ulnar neuropathy at or distal to the wrist. *Muscle Nerve*. 1988;11:828–832.

Seror P. Comparison of the distal motor latency of the first dorsal interosseous with abductor pollicis brevis. *Electromyogr clin Neurophysiol*. 1988;28:341–345.

CHAPTER 2

UPPER LIMB SENSORY AND MIXED NERVE STUDIES

LATERAL ANTEBRACHIAL CUTANEOUS SENSORY NERVE

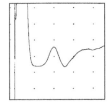

Typical waveform
appearance

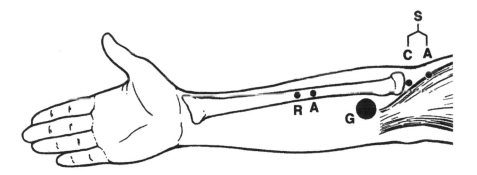

Electrode Placement

Position: This study is performed in the supine position.

Recording electrodes: A 3 cm bar electrode is placed on the lateral aspect of the forearm, in line with the long axis of the forearm, with the active electrode (A) 10 cm distal to the stimulation point. The reference electrode (R) is distal.

Ground electrode (G): Placement is on the mid-volar aspect of the proximal forearm.

Stimulation point (S): The cathode (C) is placed just lateral to the distal biceps tendon, with the anode (A) proximal.

Machine settings: Sensitivity—5–10 µV/division, Low frequency filter—20 Hz, High frequency filter—2 kHz, Sweep speed—1 msec/division.

Nerve fibers tested: C5 and C6 nerve roots, through the upper trunk, anterior division, and lateral cord of the brachial plexus. This sensory branch is the continuation of the musculocutaneous nerve.

Reference values (1) (213 subjects) (skin temperature over the dorsum of the hand greater than or equal to 32°C):

Onset latency (msec)

Mean	SD	Range	Upper Reference Value
1.7	0.2	1.3–2.3	2.1

Peak latency (msec)

Mean	SD	Range	Upper Reference Value
2.2	0.2	1.6–2.8	2.5

Onset to peak amplitude (µV)

Mean	SD	Range	Lower Reference Value
18	10	4–56	5

Peak to peak amplitude (µV)

Mean	SD	Lower Reference Value
22	15	6

Area under the curve from onset to positive peak (μVms)

Mean	SD	Range	Lower Limit of Normal
11	7	3–44	4

Rise time from onset to negative peak (msec)

Mean	SD	Range	Upper Limit of Normal
0.5	0.1	0.2–0.7	0.6

Duration from onset to positive peak (msec)

Mean	SD	Range	Upper Limit of Normal
1.1	0.2	0.7–1.7	1.5

Acceptable Differences

The upper limit of normal increase in onset latency from one side to the other is 0.2 msec.

The upper limit of normal increase in peak latency from one side to the other is 0.3 msec.

The upper limit of normal decrease in onset to peak amplitude from one side to the other is 69%.

The upper limit of normal decrease in peak-to-peak amplitude from one side to the other is 68%.

The upper limit of normal difference between medial antebrachial cutaneous and lateral antebrachial cutaneous onset and peak latency in the same limb is 0.3 msec in cases where the medial antebrachial cutaneous has the longer latency; it is also 0.3 msec in cases where the lateral antebrachial cutaneous latency is longer (2).

Helpful Hints

- When compared with the medial antebrachial cutaneous nerve study, the lateral antebrachial nerve generally has a larger amplitude.

- The cathode should be placed immediately next to the biceps tendon to obtain an optimal recording. Slight pressure may be necessary.

Notes _____

_____

_____

_____

_____

_____

_____

_____

REFERENCES

1. Buschbacher R, Koch J, Emsley C, Katz B. Electrodiagnostic reference values for the lateral antebrachial cutaneous nerve: standardization of a 10-cm distance. *Arch Phys Med Rehabil.* 2000;81(12):1563–1566.
2. Prahlow ND, Buschbacher RM. An antidromic study of the medial antebrachial cutaneous nerve, with a comparison of the differences between medial and lateral antebrachial cutaneous nerve latencies. *J Long Term Eff Med Implants.* 2006;16(5):369–376.

ADDITIONAL READINGS

Izzo KL, Aravabhumi S, Jafri A, et al. Medial and lateral antebrachial cutaneous nerves: standardization of technique, reliability and age effect on healthy subjects. *Arch Phys Med Rehabil.* 1985;66:592–597.

Kimura I, Ayyar DR. Sensory nerve conduction study in the medial antebrachial cutaneous nerve. *Tohoku J Exp Med.* 1984;142:461–466.

Oishi C, Sonoo M, Kurono H, et al. A new pitfall in a sensory conduction study of the lateral antebrachial cutaneous nerve: spread to the radial nerve. *Muscle Nerve.* 2014;50(2):186–192.

Spindler HA, Felsenthal G. Sensory conduction in the musculocutaneous nerve. *Arch Phys Med Rehabil.* 1978;59:20–23.

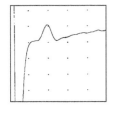

Typical waveform
appearance

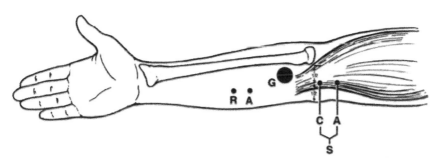

Electrode Placement

Position: This study is performed in the supine position.

Recording electrodes: A 3 cm bar electrode is placed on the medial aspect of the forearm, in line with the long axis of the forearm, so that the distance between the active electrode (A) and the cathode (C) is 10 cm. The reference electrode (R) is distal.

Ground electrode (G): Placement is on the mid-volar aspect of the forearm.

Stimulation point (S): The cathode (C) is placed at the midpoint between the medial epicondyle and the distal biceps tendon, with the anode (A) proximal.

Machine settings: Sensitivity—5–10 µV/division, Low frequency filter—20 Hz, High frequency filter—2 kHz, Sweep speed—1 msec/division.

Nerve fibers tested: C8 and T1 nerve roots, through the lower trunk, anterior division, and medial cord of the brachial plexus.

Reference values (1) (207 subjects) (skin temperature over the dorsum of the hand greater than or equal to 32°C):

Onset latency (msec)

Mean	SD	Range	Upper Reference Value
1.7	0.2	1.3–2.4	2.0

Peak latency (msec)

Mean	SD	Range	Upper Reference Value
2.2	0.2	1.8–2.8	2.6

Onset to peak amplitude (µV)

Mean	SD	Range	Lower Reference Value
13	7	3–46	4

Peak-to-peak amplitude (µV)

Mean	SD	Range	Lower Reference Value
10	7	2–43	3

Area under the curve from onset to positive peak (µVms)

Mean	SD	Range	Lower Reference Value
6	3	1–25	2

Rise time (msec)

Mean	SD	Range	Upper Reference Value
0.5	0.1	0.3–0.7	0.6

Duration from onset to positive peak (msec)

Mean	SD	Range	Upper Reference Value
1.0	0.2	0.6–1.6	1.3

Acceptable Differences

The upper limit of normal increase in onset and peak latency from one side to the other is 0.3 msec.

The upper limit of normal decrease in onset to peak amplitude from one side to the other is 67%.

The upper limit of normal decrease in peak-to-peak amplitude from one side to the other is 78%.

The upper limit of normal difference between medial antebrachial cutaneous and lateral antebrachial cutaneous onset and peak latency in the same limb is 0.3 msec in cases where the medial antebrachial cutaneous has the longer latency; it is also 0.3 msec in cases where the lateral antebrachial cutaneous latency is longer.

Helpful Hints

- When compared with the medial antebrachial cutaneous nerve study, the lateral antebrachial nerve generally has a larger amplitude.

- Occasionally, motor artifact from median nerve stimulation can obscure the recording. Lowering the stimulus intensity may be helpful.

- Occasionally, stimulus artifact can interfere with the recording. Rotating the anode or moving the ground electrode to the back of the forearm may be helpful.

Notes _____

_____

_____

_____

_____

_____

_____

_____

_____

_____

_____

REFERENCE

1. Prahlow ND, Buschbacher RM. An antidromic study of the medial antebrachial cutaneous nerve, with a comparison of the differences between medial and lateral antebrachial cutaneous nerve latencies. *J Long Term Eff Med Implants*. 2006;16(5):369–376.

ADDITIONAL READINGS

Izzo KL, Aravabhumi S, Jafri A, et al. Medial and lateral antebrachial cutaneous nerves: standardization of technique, reliability and age effect on healthy subjects. *Arch Phys Med Rehabil*. 1985;66:592–597.

Jung MJ, Byun HY, Lee CH, et al. Medial antebrachial cutaneous nerve injury after brachial plexus block: two case reports. *Ann Rehabil Med*. 2013;37(6):913–918.

Kimura I, Ayyar DR. Sensory nerve conduction study in the medial antebrachial cutaneous nerve. *Tohoku J Exp Med*. 1984;142:461–466.

Seror P. The medial antebrachial cutaneous nerve: antidromic and orthodromic conduction studies. *Muscle Nerve*. 2002;26:421–423.

MEDIAN NERVE

MEDIAN SENSORY NERVE TO THE SECOND AND THIRD DIGITS

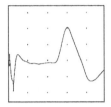

Typical waveform
appearance

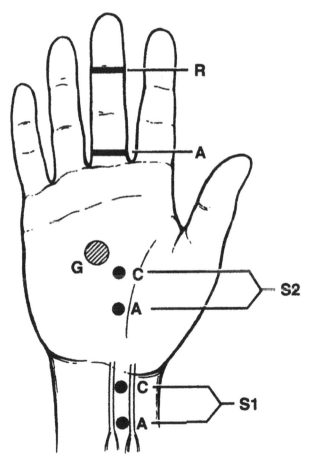

Electrode Placement

Position: This study is performed in the supine position.

Active electrode (A): A ring or clip electrode is placed in contact with the radial and ulnar sides of the digit being tested, halfway between the webspace and the proximal interphalangeal (PIP) joint.

Reference electrode (R): A ring or clip electrode is placed in contact with the radial and ulnar sides of the digit being tested, preferably at least 4 cm distal to the active electrode.

Ground electrode (G): Placement is on the dorsum of the hand.

Stimulation point 1 (S1): The subject is asked to straighten the fingers. The cathode (C) is placed 14 cm proximal to the active electrode over the median nerve at the wrist, between the tendons of the flexor carpi radialis and the palmaris longus (if the palmaris longus is absent, stimulation is applied slightly medial to the flexor carpi radialis tendon). The anode (A) is proximal.

Stimulation point 2 (S2): The cathode (C) is placed at the midpoint of the line from the active electrode to stimulation point 1. The anode (A) is proximal.

Machine settings: Sensitivity—20 µV/division, Low frequency filter—20 Hz, High frequency filter—2 kHz, Sweep speed—1 msec/division.

Nerve fibers tested: C6 (second digit) and C7 (third digit) nerve roots through the upper and middle trunks, anterior divisions, and lateral cord of the brachial plexus.

Reference values: (1) (258 subjects) (skin temperature over the dorsum of the hand 32°C or greater). The data presented are for the third digit; the results for the second digit are virtually identical.

Onset latencies (msec)

	Mean	SD	Range	Upper Reference Value
S1	2.7	0.3	1.8–3.6	3.2
S2	1.4	0.2	1.0–2.1	1.8

Peak latencies (msec)

	Mean	SD	Range	Upper Reference Value
S1	3.4	0.3	2.8–4.7	4.0
S2	2.0	0.4	1.6–2.6	2.4

Onset to peak amplitude (μV) The data are divided into groups according to age and body mass index (BMI), kg/m^2 (see Appendix 2).

		Mean	SD	Range	Lower Reference Value
S1					
	Age Range 19–49				
	BMI <24	51	19		19
	BMI ≥24	45	19		15
	Age Range 50–79				
	BMI <24	30	10		13
	BMI ≥24	24	10		8
	All subjects	41	20	6–107	10

Peak-to-peak amplitude (μV) The data are divided into groups according to age and BMI, kg/m^2 (see Appendix 2).

		Mean	SD	Range	Lower Reference Value
S1					
	Age Range 19–49				
	BMI <24	82	33		27
	BMI ≥24	69	31		19
	Age Range 50–79				
	BMI <24	47	16		18
	BMI ≥24	34	16		8
	All subjects	63	33	4–174	12

Area under the curve from onset to positive peak (μVms) The data are divided into groups according to age and BMI, kg/m² (see Appendix 2).

		Mean	SD	Range	Lower Reference Value
S1					
	Age Range 19–49				
	BMI <24	65	31		22
	BMI ≥24	53	27		18
	Age Range 50–79				
	BMI <24	37	15		15
	BMI ≥24	27	13		9
	All subjects	49	29	8–138	13

Rise time (msec)

	Mean	SD	Range	Upper Reference Value
S1	0.7	0.1	0.5–1.4	1.0
S2	0.6	0.3	0.2–0.9	0.8

Duration from onset to positive peak (msec)

	Mean	SD	Range	Upper Reference Value
S1	2.1	0.4	1.0–3.4	2.9
S2	1.8	0.5	0.6–6.2	2.7

Acceptable Differences

The upper limit of normal increase in onset and peak latency from one side to the other is 0.4 msec.

The upper limit of normal decrease in onset to peak amplitude from one side to the other is 51%.

The upper limit of normal decrease in peak-to-peak amplitude from one side to the other is 55%.

The upper limit of normal decrease in area from one side to the other is 63%.

The upper limit of normal percentage of the S1 onset latency attributable to the wrist-to-palm segment (S1 minus S2/S1) is 58%.

The upper limit of normal percentage of the S1 peak latency attributable to the wrist-to-palm segment (S1 minus S2/S1) is 50%.

The upper limit of normal increase in onset to peak and peak-to-peak amplitude from S1 to S2 is approximately 50%.

The upper limit of normal increase in latency from digit 2 to digit 3 is 0.4 msec for onset latency and 0.3 msec for peak latency.

The upper limit of normal increase in latency from digit 3 to digit 2 is 0.2 msec for onset and peak latency.

The upper limit of normal decrease in onset to peak amplitude from one digit to the other is approximately 44% to 48%.

The upper limit of normal decrease in peak-to-peak amplitude from one digit to the other is approximately 50%.

The upper limit of normal decrease in area from one digit to the other is approximately 40% to 50%.

The upper limit of normal difference between median (digit 3) and ulnar (digit 5) sensory onset latency in the same limb is 0.5 msec in cases where the median has the longer latency; it is 0.3 msec in cases where the ulnar latency is longer (2).

The upper limit of normal difference between median (digit 3) and ulnar (digit 5) sensory peak latency in the same limb is 0.4 msec in cases where the median has the longer latency; it is 0.5 msec in cases where the ulnar latency is longer (2).

Helpful Hints

- After applying the clip electrodes to the digits, they should be rotated from side-to-side to help spread the electrode paste.

- Volume conduction from the muscles of the hand may be seen as a motor wave, usually slightly after the sensory response. If this is obscuring the sensory recording, the active and recording electrodes may need to be repositioned slightly more distal on the digit. In the case of an absent sensory response, the examiner may misidentify the motor response as a delayed sensory recording.

- Asking the patient to voluntarily spread the fingers apart also reduces motor artifact.

- If there is doubt about whether the observed recording is truly a sensory response, the recording and stimulating electrodes may need to be reversed to perform an orthodromic recording. If this is done, the evoked response amplitudes can be expected to be smaller than with digital recording. Such responses may need to be averaged or even recorded with near nerve needle recording.

- If the skin of the palm is thick, it can make the S2 response difficult to elicit. Mild abrasion of the skin or needle stimulation may be needed.

- To avoid contamination of the response by contact of the clips with the adjacent fingers, a small roll of gauze may be placed between the digits to hold them apart.

- In persons with short hands, the normal 7 cm S2 site may be situated over the wrist rather than in the palm. In such cases, S2 may be moved more distally. This will still allow amplitude comparison from S1 to S2, but not latency comparison. Alternatively, S1 may be placed 12 cm proximal to the active electrode and S2 would be at 6 cm. This will still allow a latency ratio comparison.

- Stimulation can be applied across the wrist in 1 cm increments in the so-called "inching" technique. Normally, as the stimulus is applied 1 cm more distally the latency increases by 0.16–0.21 msec per 1 cm increment. Greater incremental latency changes can help to localize focal slowing (3). Incremental latencies of 0.4 msec and 0.5 msec, or a doubling of the adjacent segments' latencies, have been recommended as reference values (4,5). Ross and Kimura recommend that inching be done not to diagnose carpal tunnel syndrome, but to confirm the site of slowing (6).

- Comparing the distal and proximal segments of the median sensory study (S2 and S1) can be used to distinguish between median mononeuropathy at the wrist and peripheral polyneuropathy. The distal segment is obtained by antidromic stimulation in the palm with recording at the index finger or middle finger. Stimulation is 7 or 8 cm from the wrist stimulation, usually between the second and third metacarpals. In median mononeuropathy the maximal slowing is across the wrist whereas in peripheral neuropathy both the distal and proximal segments are abnormal. With regards to amplitude a >50% reduction in the proximal segment compared to the distal suggests conduction block (7–9).

- The median to ulnar sensory peak latency difference for active workers, comparing digit 2 to digit 5 is normally ≤0.8 ms (10).

- The median to ulnar sensory peak latency difference for mild diabetics, comparing digit 2 to digit 5 is normally ≤1.0 ms (11).

Notes

REFERENCES

1. Buschbacher RM. Median 14 cm and 7 cm antidromic sensory studies to digits 2 and 3. *Am J Phys Med Rehabil*. 1999;78:S53–S62.

2. Grossart EA, Prahlow ND, Buschbacher RM. Acceptable differences in sensory and motor latencies between the median and ulnar nerves. *J Long Term Eff Med Implants*. 2006;16(5):395–400.

3. Kimura J. The carpal tunnel syndrome: localization of conduction abnormalities within the distal segment of the median nerve. *Brain*. 1979;102:619–635.

4. Nathan PA, Keniston RC, Meadows KD, Lockwood RS. Predictive value of nerve conduction measurements at the carpal tunnel. *Muscle Nerve*. 1993;16:1377–1382.

5. Nathan PA, Meadows KD, Doyle LS. Sensory segmental latency values of the median nerve for a population of normal individuals. *Arch Phys Med Rehabil*. 1988;69:499–501.

6. Ross MA, Kimura J. AAEM case report #2: the carpal tunnel syndrome. *Muscle Nerve*. 1995;18:567–573.

7. Stevens JC. AAEE minimonograph #26: the electrodiagnosis of carpal tunnel syndrome. *Muscle Nerve*. 1987;10:99–113.

8. Stevens JC. AAEM minimonograph #26: the electrodiagnosis of carpal tunnel syndrome. *Muscle Nerve*. 1997;20:1477–1486.

9. Ross MA, Kimura J. AAEM case report #2: the carpal tunnel syndrome. *Muscle Nerve*. 1995;18:567–573.

10. Salerno DF, Franzblau A, Werner RA, et al. Median to ulnar nerve conduction studies for active workers: normative values. *Muscle Nerve*. 1998;21:999–1005.

11. Albers JW, Brown MB, Sima AA, Greene DA. Frequency of median mononeuropathy in patients with mild diabetic neuropathy in the early diabetes intervention trial (EDIT). Tolerstat study group for EDIT. *Muscle Nerve*. 1996;19:140–146.

ADDITIONAL READINGS

Falco FJE, Hennessey WJ, Braddom RL, Goldberg G. Standardized nerve conduction studies in the upper limb of the healthy elderly. *Am J Phys Med Rehabil.* 1992;71:263–271.

Felsenthal G. Median and ulnar distal motor and sensory latencies in the same normal subject. *Arch Phys Med Rehabil.* 1977;58:297–302.

Felsenthal G, Spindler H. Palmar conduction time of median and ulnar nerves of normal subjects and patients with carpal tunnel syndrome. *Am J Phys Med Rehabil.* 1979;58:131–138.

Hennessey WJ, Falco FJE, Braddom RL. Median and ulnar nerve conduction studies: normative data for young adults. *Arch Phys Med Rehabil.* 1994;75:259–264.

Hennessey WJ, Falco FJE, Goldberg G, Braddom RL. Gender and arm length: influence on nerve conduction parameters in the upper limb. *Arch Phys Med Rehabil.* 1994;75:265–269.

Melvin JL, Schuchmann JA, Lanese RR. Diagnostic specificity of motor and sensory nerve conduction variables in the carpal tunnel syndrome. *Arch Phys Med Rehabil.* 1973;54:69–74.

Monga TN, Shanks GL, Poole BJ. Sensory palmar stimulation in the diagnosis of carpal tunnel syndrome. *Arch Phys Med Rehabil.* 1985;66:598–600.

Wongsam PE, Johnson EW, Weinerman JD. Carpal tunnel syndrome: use of palmar stimulation of sensory fibers. *Arch Phys Med Rehabil.* 1983;64:16–19.

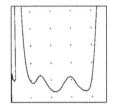

Typical waveform
appearance

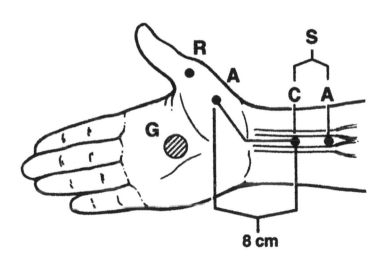

8 cm

Electrode Placement

Position: This study is performed in the supine position. Set-up is as for median motor nerve conduction to the abductor pollicis brevis.

Active electrode (A): Placement is halfway between the midpoint of the distal wrist crease and the 1st metacarpophalangeal joint.

Reference electrode (R): Placement is slightly distal to the 1st metacarpophalangeal joint.

Ground electrode (G): Placement is on the dorsum of the hand. If stimulus artifact interferes with the recording, the ground may be placed near the active electrode, between this electrode and the cathode.

Stimulation point (S): The cathode (C) is placed 8 cm proximal to the active electrode, in a line measured first to the midpoint of the distal wrist crease and then to a point slightly ulnar to the tendon of the flexor carpi radialis. The anode (A) is proximal.

Machine settings: Sensitivity—10 μV/division, Low frequency filter—20 Hz, High frequency filter 2 kHz, Sweep speed—1 msec/division.

Nerve fibers tested: C6 nerve root through the upper trunk, anterior division, and lateral cord of the brachial plexus. This branch leaves the median nerve above the carpal tunnel.

Reference values (1) (10 subjects) (temperature not reported):

Peak latency (msec)

Mean	SD	Range	Upper Reference Value
1.54	0.08	1.38–1.70	1.70

Peak-to-peak amplitude (μV)

Mean	SD
9.03	10.58

Helpful Hints

- There are two small amplitude negative waves preceding the compound motor action potential of the abductor pollicis brevis. Both waves should be visualized using the technique described in the preceding section. This will enable the examiner to correctly identify the sensory nerve action potential (SNAP) of the median palmar cutaneous nerve, which is the first of the two small amplitude negative waves. The second negative wave is a far field recording of either the junctional potential of the median digital nerve entering the thumb or that of a fixed neural generator in the palm.

- The cathode may be repositioned laterally to attempt to selectively depolarize the median palmar cutaneous nerve. Using a short duration stimulus may decrease the recording interference from the stimulus artifact. Using a submaximal stimulus intensity from that used to record the motor response may also be helpful. Repositioning of the active electrode proximally may also be helpful. The amplitude will be larger with more proximal placement and therefore may be more easily detected in some individuals. Care should be taken not to place the active electrode too far medially, as the sensory recording might be obscured by depolarization of the main median trunk.

Notes

REFERENCE

1. Bergeron JW, Braddom RL. Palmar cutaneous nerve recording and clarification of median premotor potential generators. *Am J Phys Med Rehabil.* 1998;77:399–406.

ADDITIONAL READING/ALTERNATE TECHNIQUE

Chang CW, Lien IN. Comparison of sensory nerve conduction in the palmar cutaneous branch and first digital branch of the median nerve: a new diagnostic method for carpal tunnel syndrome. *Muscle Nerve.* 1991;14:1173–1176.

POSTERIOR ANTEBRACHIAL CUTANEOUS NERVE

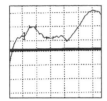

Typical waveform appearance

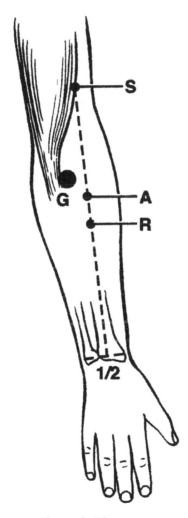

Electrode Placement

Position: This study is performed in the supine position, with the forearm pronated.

Recording electrodes: Placement is along a line from the stimulation point to the mid-dorsum of the wrist (midway between the radial and ulnar styloid processes). The active electrode (A) is placed approximately 12 cm distal to the stimulating electrode. The reference electrode (R) is 3 cm distal.

Ground electrode (G): Placement is between the stimulating and recording electrodes.

Stimulation point (S): Placement of the cathode is just above the lateral epicondyle, between the biceps and triceps. The anode is proximal.

Machine settings: Low frequency filter—5 Hz, High frequency filter—5 kHz, Sensitivity—10 µV/division, Sweep speed—1 msec/division.

Nerve fibers tested: C5–C8 nerve roots, through the upper, middle, and lower trunks, posterior divisions, and posterior cord of the brachial plexus, and then through the radial nerve.

Reference values (1) (63 subjects) (distance 12.0 cm, skin temperature 32–34°):

Onset latency (msec)

Age Range	Mean	SD	Range
20–39	2.00	0.13	
40–59	2.05	0.11	
≥60	2.19	0.17	
All subjects	2.07	0.16	1.80–2.60

Peak latency (msec)

Age Range	Mean	SD	Range
20–39	2.25	0.12	
40–59	2.34	0.13	
≥60	2.48	0.18	
All subjects	2.35	0.15	2.05–2.90

Peak to peak amplitude (µV)

Age Range	Mean	SD	Range
20–39	6.93	2.01	
40–59	6.41	2.10	

Age Range	Mean	SD	Range
≥60	4.74	1.54	
All subjects	6.10	2.11	2.90–13.00

Acceptable Difference

The study authors' suggested upper limit of normal decrease in amplitude from side-to-side is 40%.

Helpful Hints

- This nerve supplies sensation to the skin of the lateral arm and elbow and dorsal forearm to the wrist.

- The waveform may be difficult to record because of motor artifact. Lower intensity stimulation may be necessary. Adjustment of the stimulating and recording electrodes may be needed as well.

- Initially, stimulation should be performed 1/2–2 cm directly above the lateral epicondyle. If no response is obtained, the stimulator should be moved anteriorly or posteriorly.

- Stimulation may be better if done slightly closer to the triceps muscle.

Notes

REFERENCE

1. Prakash KM, Leoh TH, Dan YF, et al. Posterior antebrachial cutaneous nerve conduction studies in normal subjects. *Clinical Neurophysiology.* 2004;115:752–754.

ADDITIONAL READINGS/ALTERNATE TECHNIQUES

Ma DM, Liveson JA. *Nerve Conduction Handbook.* Philadelphia, PA: FA Davis; 1983.

Souayah N, Bhatt M, Sander HW. Posterior antebrachial cutaneous nerve conduction study technique. *Neurol Neurophysiol Neurosci.* 2007;4:5.

RADIAL SENSORY NERVE TO THE DORSUM OF THE HAND

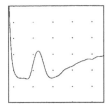

Typical waveform
appearance

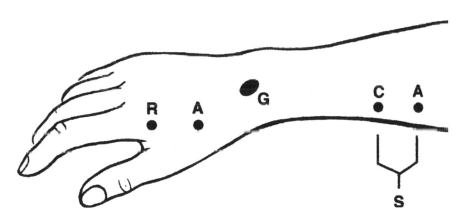

Electrode Placement

Position: This study is performed in the supine position.

Recording electrodes: A 3 cm bar is placed with the active electrode (A) over the radial sensory nerve as the nerve passes over the extensor pollicis longus tendon (this can often be palpated). The reference electrode (R) is distal.

Ground electrode (G): Placement is on the dorsum of the hand.

Stimulation point (S): The cathode (C) is placed on the radial side of the forearm 10 cm proximal to the active electrode. The anode (A) is proximal.

Machine settings: Sensitivity—5–10 µV/division, Low frequency filter—20 Hz, High frequency filter—2 kHz, Sweep speed—1 msec/division.

Nerve fibers tested: C6 nerve root, through the upper trunk, posterior division, posterior cord of the brachial plexus, and then through the radial nerve.

Reference values (1) (212 subjects) (skin temperature over the dorsum of the hand greater than or equal to 32°C):

Onset latency (msec)

Mean	SD	Range	Upper Reference Value
1.9	0.2	1.4–2.4	2.2

Peak latency (msec)

Mean	SD	Range	Upper Reference Value
2.4	0.2	1.9–3.1	2.8

Onset to peak amplitude (µV)

Mean	SD	Range	Lower Reference Value
29	13	4–75	7

Peak-to-peak amplitude (µV)

Mean	SD	Range	Lower Reference Value
33	14	4–92	11

Area under the curve from onset to positive peak (μVms)

Mean	SD	Range	Lower Reference Value
18	7	3–47	6

Rise time (msec)

Mean	SD	Range	Upper Reference Value
0.5	0.1	0.2–0.8	0.7

Duration from onset to positive peak (msec)

Mean	SD	Range	Upper Reference Value
1.2	0.2	0.9–2.6	1.6

Acceptable Differences

The upper limit of normal increase in onset and peak latency from one side to the other is 0.3 msec.

The upper limit of normal decrease in onset to peak amplitude from one side to the other is 64%.

The upper limit of normal decrease in peak-to-peak amplitude from one side to the other is 54%.

The upper limit of normal difference between radial and dorsal ulnar cutaneous onset latency in the same limb is 0.5 msec in cases where the radial has the longer latency; it is 0.3 msec in cases where the dorsal ulnar cutaneous latency is longer.

The upper limit of normal difference between radial and dorsal ulnar cutaneous peak latency in the same limb is 0.4 msec in cases where the radial has the longer latency; it is also 0.4 msec in cases where the dorsal ulnar cutaneous latency is longer.

Helpful Hint

- Asking the subject to actively extend the thumb may help in palpating and localizing the nerve.

Notes

_____

_____

_____

_____

_____

_____

_____

_____

REFERENCE

1. Evanoff V, Buschbacher RM. Radial versus dorsal ulnar sensory studies. *J Long Term Eff Med Implants*. 2006;16(5):349–358.

ADDITIONAL READINGS

Chang CW, Oh SJ. Sensory nerve conduction study in forearm segment of superficial radial nerve: standardization of technique. *Electromyogr Clin Neurophysiol*. 1990;30:349–351.

Hoffman MD, Mitz M, Luisi M, Melville BR. Paired study of the dorsal cutaneous ulnar and superficial radial sensory nerves. *Arch Phys Med Rehabil*. 1988;69:591–594.

Mackenzie K, DeLisa JA. Distal sensory latency measurement of the superficial radial nerve in normal adult subjects. *Arch Phys Med Rehabil*. 1981;62:31–34.

Park BK, Bun HR, Hwang M, Hong J, Kim DH. Medial and lateral branches of the superficial radial nerve: cadaver and nerve conduction studies. *Clin Neurophysiol*. 2010;121(2):228–232.

ULNAR NERVE

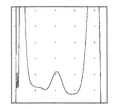

Typical waveform
appearance

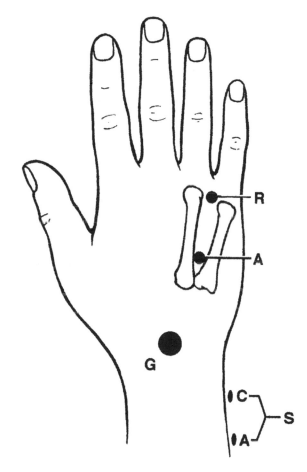

Electrode Placement

Position: This study is performed in the supine position, with elbow flexed to 90°.

Recording electrodes: A 3 cm bar is placed with the active electrode (A) in the "V" formed by the proximal dorsal 4th and 5th metacarpals. The reference electrode (R) is distal.

Ground electrode (G): Placement is on the dorsum of the hand.

Stimulation point (S): The cathode (C) is placed 10 cm proximal to the active electrode over the ulna or between the ulna and the flexor carpi ulnaris. The anode (A) is proximal.

Machine settings: Sensitivity—5–10 µV/division, Low frequency filter—20 Hz, High frequency filter—2 kHz, Sweep speed—1 msec/division.

Nerve fibers tested: C8 nerve root, through the lower trunk, anterior division, medial cord of the brachial plexus, and ulnar nerve.

Reference values (1) (194 subjects) (skin temperature over the dorsum of the hand greater than or equal to 32°C):

Onset latency (msec)

Mean	SD	Range	Upper Reference Value
1.8	0.3	1.2–4.5	2.3

Peak latency (msec)

Mean	SD	Range	Upper Reference Value
2.3	0.4	1.8–6.1	2.9

Onset to peak amplitude (µV)

Mean	SD	Range	Lower Reference Value
17	10	4–50	5

Peak-to-peak amplitude (µV)

Mean	SD	Range	Lower Reference Value
20	13	5–76	5

Area under the curve from onset to positive peak (μVms)

Mean	SD	Range	Lower Reference Value
11	7	3–43	3

Rise time (msec)

Mean	SD	Range	Upper Reference Value
0.5	0.1	0.2–1.6	0.8

Duration from onset to positive peak (msec)

Mean	SD	Range	Upper Reference Value
1.2	0.2	0.8–2.6	1.6

Acceptable Differences

The upper limit of normal increase in onset latency from one side to the other is 0.5 msec.

The upper limit of normal increase in peak latency from one side to the other is 0.4 msec.

The upper limit of normal decrease in onset to peak amplitude from one side to the other is 59%.

The upper limit of normal decrease in peak-to-peak amplitude from one side to the other is 67%.

The upper limit of normal difference between radial and dorsal ulnar cutaneous onset latency in the same limb is 0.5 msec in cases where the radial has the longer latency; it is 0.3 msec in cases where the dorsal ulnar cutaneous latency is longer.

The upper limit of normal difference between radial and dorsal ulnar cutaneous peak latency in the same limb is 0.4 msec in cases where the radial has the longer latency; it is also 0.4 msec in cases where the dorsal ulnar cutaneous latency is longer.

Helpful Hints

- Anomalous innervation to this area may be present.

- This sensory recording is often obscured by motor artifact, especially if the waveform is delayed. Submaximal stimulation can be useful if this is the case.

- Kim and coworkers reported that if difficulty was encountered in obtaining a response, the following maneuvers can be used: (a) stimulator can be moved 2–3 cm more proximal or distal, (b) an orthodromic technique can be used, and (c) the radial and musculocutaneous nerves can be stimulated to test for an anomalous innervation pattern (2).

- Hoffman and coworkers reported that supinating the forearm produced better recordings (3).

Notes

REFERENCES

1. Evanoff V, Buschbacher RM. Radial sensory versus dorsal ulnar sensory studies. *J Long Term Eff Med Implants.* 2006;16(5):349–358.
2. Kim DJ, Kalantri A, Guha S, Wainapel SF. Dorsal cutaneous ulnar nerve conduction. *Arch Neurol.* 1981; 38:321–322.
3. Hoffman MD, Mitz M, Luisi M, Melville BR. Paired study of the dorsal cutaneous ulnar and superficial radial sensory nerves. *Arch Phys Med Rehabil.* 1988;69:591–594.

ADDITIONAL READINGS

Jabre JF. Ulnar nerve lesions at the wrist: new technique for recording from the sensory dorsal branch of the ulnar nerve. *Neurology* 1980;30:873–876.
Young SH, Kalantri A. Dorsal ulnar cutaneous nerve conduction studies in an asymptomatic population (abstract). *Arch Phys Med Rehabil.* 1998;79:1166.

ULNAR SENSORY NERVE TO THE FIFTH DIGIT

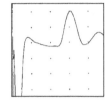

Typical waveform
appearance

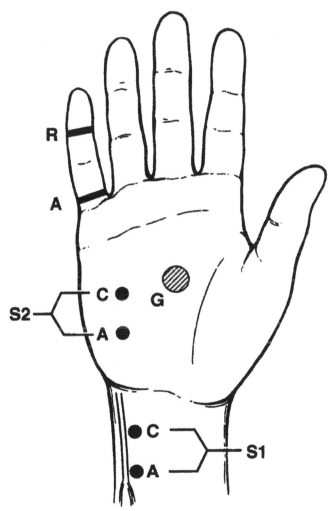

Electrode Placement

Position: This study is performed in the supine position.

Active electrode (A): A ring or clip electrode is placed in contact with the radial and ulnar sides of the fifth digit, midway between the webspace and the PIP joint.

Reference electrode (R): A ring or clip electrode is placed in contact with the radial and ulnar sides of the fifth digit, 4 cm distal to the active electrode (or in small fingers as far distally as possible).

Ground electrode (G): Placement is on the dorsum of the hand.

Stimulation point 1 (S1): The subject is asked to straighten the fingers. The cathode (C) is placed 14 cm proximal to the active electrode over the ulnar nerve at the wrist, slightly radial to the tendon of the flexor carpi ulnaris. The anode (A) is proximal.

Stimulation point 2 (S2): The cathode (C) is placed at the midpoint of the line from the active electrode to stimulation point 1. The anode (A) is proximal.

Machine settings: Sensitivity—20 µV/division, Low frequency filter—20 Hz, High frequency filter—2 kHz, Sweep speed—1 msec/division.

Nerve fibers tested: C8 nerve root, through the lower trunk, anterior division, medial cord of the brachial plexus, and ulnar nerve.

Reference values (1) (258 subjects) (skin temperature over the dorsum of the hand 32°C or greater):

Onset latencies (msec)

	Mean	SD	Range	Upper Reference Value
S1	2.6	0.2	2.0–3.3	3.1
S2	1.4	0.2	0.9–1.9	1.8

Peak latencies (msec)

	Mean	SD	Range	Upper Reference Value
S1	3.4	0.3	2.7–4.8	4.0
S2	2.0	0.2	1.6–2.8	2.5

Onset to peak amplitude (μV) The data are divided into groups according to age and BMI, kg/m² (see Appendix 2).

	Mean	SD	Range	Lower Reference Value
S1				
Age Range 19–49				
BMI <24	43	17		14
BMI ≥24	36	16		11
Age Range 50–79				
BMI <24	27	11		10
BMI ≥24	20	9		5
All subjects	33	17	1–85	6

Peak-to-peak amplitude (μV) The data are divided into groups according to age and BMI, kg/m² (see Appendix 2).

	Mean	SD	Range	Lower Reference Value
S1				
Age Range 19–49				
BMI <24	70	36		13
BMI ≥24	54	31		8
Age Range 50–79				
BMI <24	37	13		13
BMI ≥24	27	15		4
All subjects	50	32	1–179	4

Area under the curve from onset to positive peak (μVms) The data are divided into groups according to age and BMI, kg/m² (see Appendix 2).

	Mean	SD	Range	Lower Reference Value
S1				
Age Range 19–49				
BMI <24	53	29		14
BMI ≥24	38	22		10

	Mean	SD	Range	Lower Reference Value
Age Range 50–79				
BMI <24	28	11		12
BMI ≥24	22	14		6
All subjects	37	24	3–138	8

Rise time (msec)

	Mean	SD	Range	Upper Reference Value
S1	0.8	0.2	0.5–2.1	1.1
S2	0.6	0.1	0.3–1.3	0.9

Duration from onset to positive peak (msec)

	Mean	SD	Range	Upper Reference Value
S1	1.9	0.4	1.0–3.5	2.7
S2	1.7	0.3	1.0–3.0	2.5

Acceptable Differences

The upper limit of normal increase in onset latency from one side to the other is 0.3 msec.

The upper limit of normal increase in peak latency from one side to the other is 0.4 msec.

The upper limit of normal decrease in onset to peak amplitude from one side to the other is 53%.

The upper limit of normal decrease in peak-to-peak amplitude from one side to the other is 64%.

The upper limit of normal decrease in area from one side to the other is 65%.

The upper limit of normal percentage of the S1 onset latency attributable to the wrist-to-palm segment (S1 minus S2/S1) is 54%.

The upper limit of normal percentage of the S1 peak latency attributable to the wrist-to-palm segment (S1 minus S2/S1) is 47%.

The upper limit of normal increase in onset to peak amplitude from S1 to S2 is 71%.

The upper limit of normal increase in peak-to-peak amplitude from S1 to S2 is 60%.

The upper limit of normal difference between median (digit 3) and ulnar (digit 5) sensory onset latency in the same limb is 0.5 msec in cases where the median has the longer latency; it is 0.3 msec in cases where the ulnar latency is longer (2).

The upper limit of normal difference between median (digit 3) and ulnar (digit 5) sensory peak latency in the same limb is 0.4 msec in cases where the median has the longer latency; it is 0.5 msec in cases where the ulnar latency is longer (2).

Helpful Hints

- After applying the clip electrodes to the digits, they should be rotated from side to side to help spread the electrode paste.

- Volume conduction from the muscles of the hand may be seen as a motor wave, usually slightly after the sensory response. If this is obscuring the sensory recording, the active and recording electrodes may need to be repositioned slightly more distal on the digit. In the case of an absent sensory response, the examiner may misidentify the motor response as a delayed sensory recording.

- If there is doubt about whether the observed recording is truly a sensory response, the recording and stimulating electrodes may need to be reversed to perform an orthodromic recording. If this is done, the evoked response amplitudes can be expected to be smaller than with digital recording. Such responses may need to be averaged or even recorded with near nerve needle recording.

- If the skin of the palm is thick, it may make the S2 response difficult to elicit. Mild abrasion of the skin or needle stimulation may be needed.

- Asking the patient to voluntarily spread the fingers apart can both reduce motor artifact and avoid contamination of the response by contact of the recording electrode with the adjacent finger.

- In persons with short hands, the normal 7 cm S2 site may be situated over the wrist rather than in the palm. In such cases, S2 may be moved more distally. This will still allow amplitude comparison from S1 to S2, but not latency comparison. Alternatively, S1 may be placed 12 cm proximal to the active electrode and S2 would be at 6 cm. This will still allow a latency ratio comparison.

- The sensory studies are usually performed only for relatively short distances. This is due to the fact that sensory compound action potentials are particularly sensitive to phase cancellation, causing a rapid decrease in amplitude with increasing distance from the recording site. One study has presented the data for sensory recording with more proximal stimulation for 20 subjects (averaging used). The mean + 2 SD value for latency change for a 10 cm segment across the elbow (see ulnar nerve motor study to the abductor digiti minimi) was 1.8 msec for onset latency and 1.9 msec for peak latency. Side-to-side difference (mean + 2 SD) in latency change across this segment was 0.6 msec for onset latency and 0.3 msec for peak latency. The upper limit of normal decrement of peak-to-peak amplitude was 74%

(range 12%–72%) across the wrist to below elbow segment and 41% (range 0%–50%) for the below to above elbow segment. The lower limits of normal nerve conduction velocity (calculated for onset latency) were 59 m/sec below the elbow and 50 m/sec across the elbow) (3).

Notes _____

_____

_____

REFERENCES

1. Buschbacher RM. Ulnar 14 cm and 7 cm antidromic sensory studies to the 5th digit. *Am J Phys Med Rehabil.* 1999;78:S63–S68.
2. Grossart EA, Prahlow ND, Buschbacher RM. Acceptable differences in sensory and motor latencies between the median and ulnar nerves. *J Long Term Eff Med Implants.* 2006;16(5):395–400.
3. Felsenthal G, Freed MJ, Kalafut R, Hilton EB. Across-elbow ulnar nerve sensory conduction technique. *Arch Phys Med Rehabil.* 1989;70:668–672.

ADDITIONAL READINGS

Falco FJE, Hennessey WJ, Braddom RL, Goldberg G. Standardized nerve conduction studies in the upper limb of the healthy elderly. *Am J Phys Med Rehabil.* 1992;71:263–271.

Hennessey WJ, Falco FJE, Braddom RL. Median and ulnar nerve conduction studies: normative data for young adults. *Arch Phys Med Rehabil.* 1994;75:259–264.

Hennessey WJ, Falco FJE, Goldberg G, Braddom RL. Gender and arm length: influence on nerve conduction parameters in the upper limb. *Arch Phys Med Rehabil.* 1994;75:265–269.

Nesathurai S, Gwardjan A, Kamath AN. Median-to-ulnar sensory nerve action potential amplitude ratio as an electrodiagnostic adjunct for carpal tunnel syndrome. *Arch Phys Med Rehabil.* 1999;80:756–759.

Salerno DF, Franzblau A, Werner RA, et al. Median and ulnar nerve conduction studies among workers: normative values. *Muscle Nerve.* 1998;21:999–1005.

Stowell ED, Gnatz SM. Ulnar palmar cutaneous nerve and hypothenar sensory conduction studies. *Arch Phys Med Rehabil.* 1992;73:842–846.

COMPARATIVE STUDIES

MEDIAN AND RADIAL SENSORY NERVES TO THE THUMB

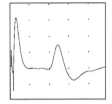

Typical waveform
appearance

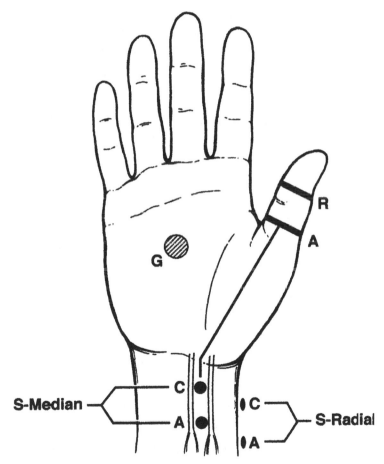

Electrode Placement

128

Position: This study is performed in the supine position, with the forearm in supination.

Active electrode (A): A ring or clip electrode is placed just distal to the first metacarpophalangeal joint.

Reference electrode (R): A ring or clip electrode is placed 4 cm distally on the thumb. For subjects with short thumbs, it is placed as far distal as possible.

Ground electrode (G): Placement is on the dorsum of the hand.

Stimulation point (S-Radial): The cathode (C) is placed 10 cm proximal to the active electrode, along the lateral border of the radius. The measurement is taken with the thumb held in line with the radius to allow measuring along the straightest line possible.

Stimulation point (S-Median): The cathode (C) is placed 10 cm proximal to the active electrode, in a line measured first to the midpoint of the distal wrist crease and then to a point slightly ulnar to the tendon of the flexor carpi radialis. The anode (A) is proximal.

Machine settings: Sensitivity—5–20 µV/division, Low frequency filter—20 Hz, High frequency filter—2 kHz, Sweep speed—1 msec/division.

Nerve fibers tested: Median: C6 nerve root through the upper trunk, anterior division, lateral cord of the brachial plexus, and median nerve. Radial: C6 nerve root through the upper trunk, posterior division, posterior cord of the brachial plexus, and radial nerve.

Reference values (1) (203 subjects) (skin temperature over the dorsum of the hand greater than or equal to 32°C):

Onset latency (msec)

	Mean	*SD*	*Range*	*Upper Reference Value*
Median	2.1	0.2	1.7–3.3	2.5
Radial	2.0	0.2	1.6–2.5	2.4

Peak latency (msec)

	Mean	*SD*	*Range*	*Upper Reference Value*
Median	2.7	0.2	2.2–3.2	3.1
Radial	2.6	0.2	2.1–3.4	3.0

Onset to peak amplitude (µV)

	Sex	Age Range	Mean	SD	Range	Lower Reference Value
Median	Female	19–49	46	14	14–79	26
		50–79	23	9	9–46	10
	Male	19–49	31	13	5–68	11
		50–79	19	8	8–39	8
	All subjects		33	16	5–79	10
Radial	All subjects		9	6	3–46	3

Peak-to-peak amplitude (µV)

	Sex	Age Range	Mean	SD	Range	Lower Limit of Normal
Median	Female	19–49	62	19	24–119	35
		50–79	33	17	9–94	12
	Male	19–49	45	25	5–117	11
		50–79	23	11	9–50	9
	All subjects		45	24	5–119	11
Radial	All subjects		12	9	3–64	4

Area (µVms-onset to positive peak)

	Sex	Age Range	Mean	SD	Range	Lower Limit of Normal
Median	Female	19–49	36	14	11–78	15
		50–79	21	12	6–63	7
	Male	19–49	28	15	4–75	5
		50–79	15	7	6–29	6
	All subjects		27	15	4–78	6
Radial	All subjects		8	6	2–37	3

Rise time (msec)

	Mean	SD	Range	Upper Limit of Normal
Median	0.6	0.1	0.3–1.2	0.8
Radial	0.6	0.1	0.2–1.0	0.9

Duration from onset to positive peak (msec)

	Mean	SD	Range	Upper Limit of Normal
Median	1.6	0.3	0.5–2.7	2.3
Radial	1.5	0.4	0.8–2.6	2.2

Acceptable Differences

The upper limit of normal difference between medial and radial peak latency in the same limb is 0.6 msec in cases where the median has the longer latency; it is 0.4 msec in cases where the radial latency is longer.

The upper limit of normal difference between medial and radial onset latency in the same limb is 0.5 msec in cases where the median has the longer latency; it is 0.3 msec in cases where the radial latency is longer.

The upper limit of normal increase in median onset latency from one side to the other is 0.3 msec.

The upper limit of normal increase in median peak latency from one side to the other is 0.4 msec.

The upper limit of normal decrease in median onset-to-peak amplitude from one side to the other is 47%.

The upper limit of normal decrease in median peak-to-peak amplitude from one side to the other is 63%.

The upper limit of normal increase in radial onset latency from one side to the other is 0.3 msec.

The upper limit of normal increase in radial peak latency from one side to the other is 0.4 msec.

The upper limit of normal decrease in radial onset-to-peak amplitude from one side to the other is 69%.

The upper limit of normal decrease in radial peak-to-peak amplitude from one side to the other is 66%.

Helpful Hints

- Thumb position can alter this measurement, and the thumb should be extended.

- The radial nerve is less prone to injury, and therefore comparing the medial to the radial sensory segments is useful in patients with concomitant ulnar nerve injury.

Notes _____

_____

_____

_____

_____

_____

_____

_____

_____

_____

_____

_____

REFERENCE

1. Berkson A, Lohman J, Buschbacher R. Comparison of median and radial sensory studies to the thumb. *J Long Term Eff Med Implants.* 2006;16(5):387–394.

ADDITIONAL READINGS

Carroll GJ. Comparison of median and radial nerve sensory latencies in the electrophysiological diagnosis of carpal tunnel syndrome. *Electroencephalogr Clin Neurophysiol.* 1987;68:101–106.

Cho DS, MacLean IC. Comparison of normal values of median, radial, and ulnar sensory latencies. *Muscle Nerve.* 1984;7:575.

DiBenedetto M, Mitz M, Klingbeil GE, Davidoff D. New criteria for sensory nerve conduction especially useful in diagnosing carpal tunnel syndrome. *Arch Phys Med Rehabil.* 1986;67:586–589.

Falco FJE, Hennessey WJ, Braddom RL, Goldberg G. Standardized nerve conduction studies in the upper limb of the healthy elderly. *Am J Phys Med Rehabil.* 1992;71:263–271.

Hennessey WJ, Falco FJE, Goldberg G, Braddom RL. Gender and arm length: influence on nerve conduction parameters in the upper limb. *Arch Phys Med Rehabil.* 1994;75:265–269.

Jackson DA, Clifford JC. Electrodiagnosis of mild carpal tunnel syndrome. *Arch Phys Med Rehabil.* 1989;70:199–204.

Johnson EW, Sipski M, Lammertse T. Median and radial sensory latencies to digit I: normal values and usefulness in carpal tunnel syndrome. *Arch Phys Med Rehabil.* 1987;68;140–141.

Kothari MJ, Rutkove SB, Caress JB, et al. Comparison of digital sensory studies in patients with carpal tunnel syndrome. *Muscle Nerve.* 1995;18:1272–1276.

Pease WS, Cannell CD, Johnson EW. Median to radial latency difference test in mild carpal tunnel syndrome. *Muscle Nerve.* 1989;12:905–909.

MEDIAN AND ULNAR MIXED NERVE STUDIES (TRANSCARPAL)

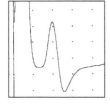

Typical waveform
appearance

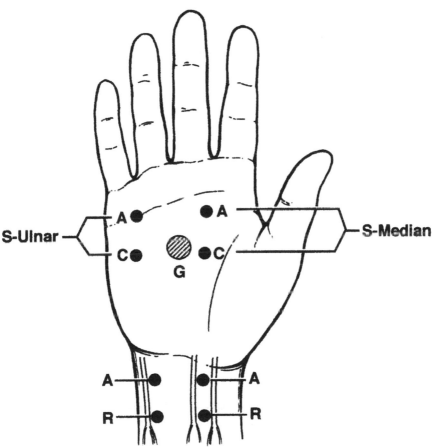

Electrode Placement

Position: This study is performed in the supine position.

Recording electrodes (median): A 3 cm bar electrode is placed with the active electrode (A) 3 cm proximal to the distal wrist crease slightly ulnar to the tendon of the flexor carpi radialis. The reference electrode (R) is proximal.

Recording electrodes (ulnar): A 3 cm bar electrode is placed with the active electrode (A) 3 cm proximal to the wrist crease slightly radial to the tendon of the flexor carpi ulnaris. The reference electrode (R) is proximal.

Ground electrode (G): Placement is on the dorsum of the hand.

Stimulation point (S-Median): The cathode (C) is placed 8 cm distal to the active electrode in the mid-palm. The anode (A) is placed distally.

Stimulation point (S-Ulnar): The cathode (C) is placed 8 cm distal to the active electrode in the lateral palm between the tendons of the flexors of the fourth and fifth digits.

Machine settings: Sensitivity—20 µV/division, Low frequency filter—20 Hz, High frequency filter—2 kHz, Sweep speed—1 msec/division.

Reference values (1) (248 subjects): (skin temperature over the dorsum of the hand at least 32°C):

Onset latencies (msec)

	Mean	SD	Range	Upper Limit of Normal
Median	1.6	0.2	1.2–2.4	2.0
Ulnar	1.6	0.2	1.2–2.0	1.9

Peak latencies (msec)

	Mean	SD	Range	Upper Limit of Normal
Median	2.1	0.2	1.6–3.1	2.4
Ulnar	2.1	0.2	1.7–2.6	2.4

Onset to peak amplitude (µV), peak-to-peak amplitude (µV), and area (µVms, onset to positive peak). The means and standard deviations were derived independently for subgroups divided by age, sex, and BMI, kg/m². The reader is directed to the reference article should this information be required. The lower limits of normal differed only for women under age 50 for the median nerve and for women under age 30 with a BMI less than 24 kg/m² for the ulnar nerve.

Lower limits of normal

	Onset-to-Peak Amplitude	Peak-to-Peak Amplitude	Area
Median			
Women under 50	27	32	17
All others	15	14	10
Ulnar			
Women under 30 with BMI under 24	22	33	14
All others	6	6	4

Rise time (msec)

	Mean	SD	Range	Upper Limit of Normal
Median	0.5	0.1	0.4–0.8	0.6
Ulnar	0.5	0.1	0.3–0.7	0.7

Duration from onset to positive peak (msec)

	Mean	SD	Range	Upper Limit of Normal
Median	1.2	0.3	0.9–4.1	1.5
Ulnar	1.2	0.2	0.7–2.0	1.5

Acceptable Differences

The upper limit of normal increase in onset or peak latency of one nerve vs. the other is 0.3 msec.

The upper limit of normal increase in onset latency from one side to the other for the median and ulnar nerves is 0.3 msec.

The upper limit of normal increase in peak latency from one side to the other is 0.3 msec for the median nerve and 0.4 msec for the ulnar nerve.

The upper limit of normal decrease in onset to peak amplitude from one side to the other is 64% for the median nerve and 73% for the ulnar nerve.

The upper limit of normal decrease in peak-to-peak amplitude from one side to the other is 64% for the median nerve and 72% for the ulnar nerve.

The upper limit of normal decrease in area from one side to the other is approximately 59% for the median nerve and 73% for the ulnar nerve.

Helpful Hints

- If a large stimulus artifact is seen, it may be helpful to rotate the stimulator.

- If stimulus is applied fairly distally in the palm, a more purely sensory response is recorded.

- If the subject's hand is small and the cathode is placed too distally to perform the technique, the bar electrode may need to be repositioned more proximally.

- The ulnar nerve waveform usually has an initial positive deflection, and the latency should be taken from this point. Difficulty in determining the "take off" can lead to errors.

Notes _____

_____

_____

_____

_____

REFERENCE

1. Buschbacher RM. Mixed nerve conduction studies of the median and ulnar nerves. *Am J Phys Med Rehabil.* 1999;78:S69–S74.

ADDITIONAL READINGS

Daube JR, Stevens JC. The electrodiagnosis of carpal tunnel syndrome (a reply). *Muscle Nerve.* 1993;16:798.

Sander HW, Quinto C, Saadeh PB, Chokroverty S. Sensitive median-ulnar motor comparative techniques in Carpal Tunnel Syndrome. *Muscle Nerve.* 1999;22:88–98.

Stevens JC: AAEM minimonograph #26: the electrodiagnosis of carpal tunnel syndrome. *Muscle Nerve.* 1997;20:1477–1486.

Stowell ED, Gnatz SM. Ulnar palmar cutaneous nerve and hypothenar sensory conduction studies. *Arch Phys Med Rehabil.* 1992;73:842–846.

Williams FH, Andary MT. *Carpal Tunnel Syndrome: Techniques for Diagnosis.* Rochester, MN: American Association of Neuromuscular and Electrodiagnostic Medicine; 2001:1–8.

MEDIAN AND ULNAR SENSORY STUDIES TO THE FOURTH DIGIT

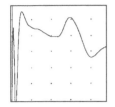

Typical waveform
appearance

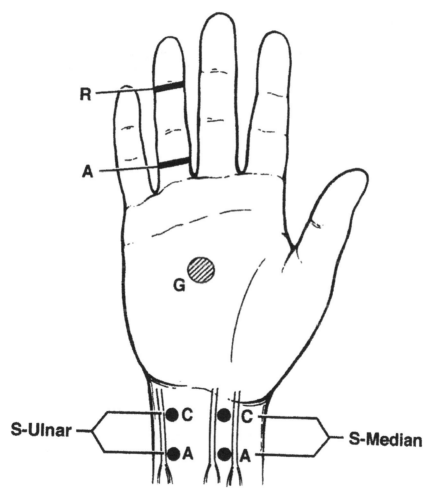

Electrode Placement

Position: This study is performed in the supine position.

Active electrode (A): A finger clip or ring electrode is placed midway between the webspace and the fourth proximal interphalangeal (PIP) joint.

Reference electrode (R): A finger clip or ring electrode is placed 4 cm distally on the same digit.

Ground electrode (G): Placement is on the dorsum of the hand.

Median stimulation point (S-Median): The cathode (C) is placed 14 cm proximal to the active electrode, slightly ulnar to the tendon of the flexor carpi radialis. The anode (A) is proximal.

Ulnar stimulation point (S-Ulnar): The cathode (C) is placed 14 cm proximal to the active electrode, slightly radial to the tendon of the flexor carpi ulnaris. The anode (A) is proximal.

Machine settings: Sensitivity—10–20 µV/division, Low frequency filter—20 Hz, High frequency filter—2 kHz, Sweep speed—1 msec/division.

Nerve fibers tested: Median: C8 nerve root through the lower trunk, anterior division, medial cord of the brachial plexus, and median nerve. Ulnar: C8 nerve root through the lower trunk, anterior division, medial cord of the brachial plexus, and ulnar nerve.

Reference values (1,3) (192 subjects) (skin temperature over the dorsum of the hand greater than or equal to 32°C):

Onset latency (msec)

	Mean	SD	Range	Upper Limit of Normal
Median	2.7	0.3	2.2–3.7	3.4
Ulnar	2.6	0.2	2.0–3.3	3.0

Peak latency (msec)

	Mean	SD	Range	Upper Limit of Normal
Median	3.4	0.3	2.7–4.8	4.1
Ulnar	3.3	0.3	2.4–4.7	3.9

Onset to peak amplitude (μV)

	Mean	SD	Range	Lower Limit of Normal
Median	21	12	4–84	5
Ulnar	23	12	4–63	5

Peak-to-peak amplitude (μV)

	Mean	SD	Range	Lower Limit of Normal
Median	34	20	4–130	10
Ulnar	36	23	4–138	10

Area under the curve from onset to positive peak (μVms)

	Mean	SD	Range	Lower Limit of Normal
Median	25	17	4–107	6
Ulnar	28	19	3–145	7

Rise time (msec)

	Mean	SD	Range	Upper Limit of Normal
Median	0.7	0.1	0.3–1.1	1.0
Radial	0.7	0.2	0.1–1.4	1.1

Duration from onset to positive peak (msec)

	Mean	SD	Range	Upper Limit of Normal
Median	1.9	0.4	1.0–2.9	2.7
Radial	1.9	0.5	0.8–3.9	2.8

Acceptable Differences

The upper limit of normal difference between median and ulnar peak latency in the same limb is 0.3 msec in cases where the ulnar latency is longer.

The upper limit of normal difference between median and ulnar onset latency in the same limb is 0.2 msec in cases where the ulnar latency is longer.

The upper limit of normal increase in median onset and peak latency from one side to the other is 0.4 msec.

The upper limit of normal decrease in median onset to peak amplitude from one side to the other is 62%.

The upper limit of normal decrease in median peak-to-peak amplitude from one side to the other is 56%.

The upper limit of normal increase in ulnar onset and peak latency from one side to the other is 0.3 msec.

The upper limit of normal decrease in ulnar onset to peak amplitude from one side to the other is 63%.

The upper limit of normal decrease in ulnar peak-to-peak amplitude from one side to the other is 73%.

The upper limit of normal difference between median and ulnar onset and peak latency in the same limb is 0.5 msec in cases where the median has the longer latency.

Helpful Hints

- This digit may be fully innervated by either the ulnar or median nerve, rather than split between the two.

- To avoid contamination of the response by contact of the ring electrodes with the adjacent fingers, a small roll of gauze may need to be placed between the digits to hold them apart. Alternatively, asking the patient to actively spread the fingers apart will do this, and also reduce motor artifact.

- The median nerve fibers to the ring finger may be more subject to compression due to the position of ring finger fibers in the outer margin of the median nerve beneath the transverse carpal ligament. Because the SNAP amplitudes are small, the median response may be absent in more severe cases of median mononeuropathy at the wrist (2).

Notes

REFERENCES

1. Berkson A, Prahlow N, Buschbacher R. Median and ulnar antidromic sensory studies to the fourth digit. *J Long Term Eff Med Implants*. 2006;16(5):377–386.
2. Werner RA, Andary M. Electrodiagnostic evaluation of carpal tunnel syndrome. *Muscle Nerve*. 2011;44:597–607.
3. Buschbacher RM, Berkson A, Mottley D, Omar Z. Median and ulnar 14 cm antidromic sensory studies to the third and fifth digits-A comparison of amplitudes. *J Long Term Eff Med Implants*. 2006;16(5):401–405.

ADDITIONAL READINGS

Cho DS, MacLean DC. Comparison of normal values of median, radial, and ulnar sensory latencies. *Muscle Nerve*. 1984;7:575.
DiBenedetto M, Mitz M, Klingbeil GE, Davidoff D. New criteria for sensory nerve conduction especially useful in diagnosing carpal tunnel syndrome. *Arch Phys Med Rehabil*. 1986;67:586–589.

Jackson DA, Clifford JC. Electrodiagnosis of mild carpal tunnel syndrome. *Arch Phys Med Rehabil.* 1989;70:199–204.

Johnson EW, Kukla RD, Wongsam PE, et al. Sensory latencies to the ring finger: normal values and relation to carpal tunnel syndrome. *Arch Phys Med Rehabil.* 1981;62:206–208.

Uncini A, Lange DJ, Solomon M, et al. Ring finger testing in carpal tunnel syndrome: a comparative study of diagnostic utility. *Muscle Nerve.* 1989;12:735–741.

COMBINED SENSORY INDEX

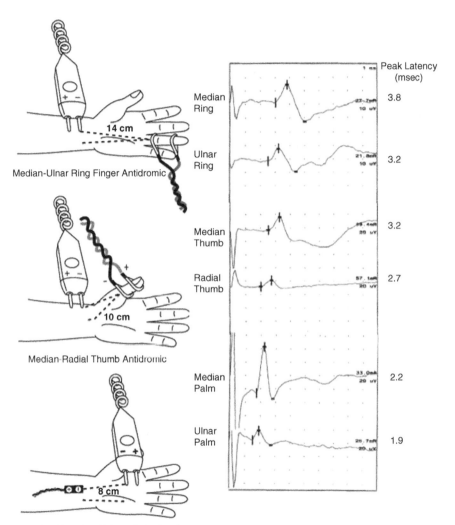

Median-Ulnar Ring Finger Antidromic

Median-Radial Thumb Antidromic

Median-Ulnar Mid-Palmar Orthodromic

	Peak Latency (msec)
Median Ring	3.8
Ulnar Ring	3.2
Median Thumb	3.2
Radial Thumb	2.7
Median Palm	2.2
Ulnar Palm	1.9

The three studies described here may be combined into a single summary number (or index) to evaluate for carpal tunnel syndrome (1). The combined sensory index is calculated by adding the three latency differences as follows:

- Median peak latency minus radial peak latency to the thumb.

- Median peak latency minus ulnar peak latency on transcarpal mixed nerve studies.

- Median peak latency minus ulnar peak latency to the fourth digit.

- When adding these three values together, the upper limit of normal is 0.9 msec.

By combining these three studies together, rather than evaluating them separately, one improves sensitivity and reduces false positive results (1). Reliability is also improved (2).

REFERENCES

1. Robinson LR, Micklesen PJ, Wang L. Strategies for analyzing nerve conduction data: superiority of a summary index over single tests. *Muscle Nerve.* 1998;21:1166–1171.
2. Lew HL, Wang L, Robinson LR. Test-retest reliability of the combined sensory index: implications for diagnosing carpal tunnel syndrome. *Muscle Nerve.* 2000; 23(8):1261–1264.

CHAPTER 3

LOWER LIMB MOTOR NERVE STUDIES

Typical waveform
appearance

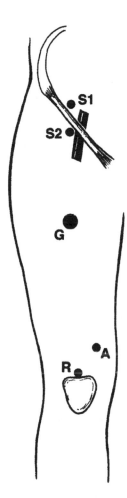

Electrode Placement

Position: This study is performed in the supine position.

Active electrode (A): Placement is over the center of the vastus medialis.

Reference electrode (R): Placement is over the quadriceps tendon just proximal to the patella (1). Placement over the patella has also been described (2).

Ground electrode (G): Placement is between the stimulating and recording electrodes.

Stimulation point 1 (S1): A monopolar needle electrode is used as the cathode for all but the thinnest subjects (2). It is ideally placed using ultrasound guidance. The stimulus is applied superior to the inguinal ligament just lateral to the femoral artery. To enhance travel of the electric field to deeper structures, the anode is under the buttock.

Stimulation point 2 (S2): A needle electrode is used as well, placed under ultrasound guidance, but inferior to the inguinal ligament and lateral to the femoral artery.

Machine settings: Sensitivity—1 mV/division, sweep speed—2 msec/division, Low frequency filter—2 to 3 Hz, High frequency filter—10 kHz

Nerve fibers tested: L2, L3, and L4 nerve roots, through the posterior division of the lumbosacral plexus and femoral nerve.

Reference values (1) (100 subjects), temperature not reported:

Latency for stimulation above ligament (msec)

Mean	SD	Range	Upper Reference Value
7.1	0.7	6.1–8.4	8.4

Latency for stimulation below ligament (msec)

Mean	SD	Range	Upper Reference Value
6.0	0.7	5.5–7.5	7.4

Delay across inguinal ligament (msec)

Mean	SD	Range	Upper Reference Value
1.1	0.4	0.8–1.8	1.8

Amplitude (mV) (2)

> *Range*
> 0.2–11.0

Helpful Hints

- Too low a stimulus intensity may result in an H-reflex being elicited.

- In the cited reference, only 75 of 100 studies were included in the final results because satisfactory recordings were not obtained in all subjects. Certain portions of the study for the remaining 25 studies were also used. The subjects were not true "normals." The data were derived using surface stimulation (1).

- Proper stimulator placement can be confirmed by ultrasound and by observing contraction of quadriceps.

- The length of the femoral nerve segment in the cited reference was 35.4 ± 1.9 cm (range 29–38).

- The distance between stimulation point above and below the inguinal ligament in the cited reference was 5.5 ± 1.6 cm (range 4.2–6.6).

- Calculation of reference values using mean + 2 SD (as done in the cited reference) may produce misleading results when distributions are skewed.

Notes _____

_____

_____

_____

_____

_____

_____

_____

REFERENCES

1. Johnson EW, Wood PK, Powers JJ. Femoral nerve conduction studies. *Arch Phys Med Rehabil.* 1968;49:528–532.

2. Kraft GH, Johnson EW. *Proximal Motor Nerve Conduction and Late Responses: An AAEM Workshop.* Rochester, MN: American Association of Electrodiagnostic Medicine; 1986.

ADDITIONAL READING/ALTERNATE TECHNIQUE

Uludag B, Ertekin C, Turman AB, et al. Proximal and distal motor nerve conduction in obturator and femoral nerves. *Arch Phys Med Rehabil.* 2000;81(9):1166–1170.

FIBULAR NERVE

FIBULAR MOTOR NERVE TO THE EXTENSOR DIGITORUM BREVIS

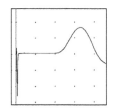

Typical waveform appearance

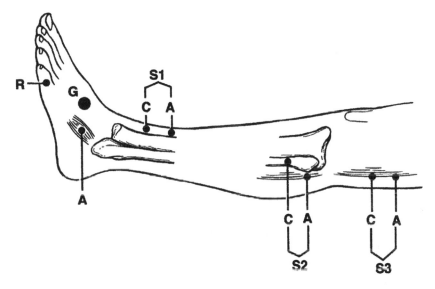

Electrode Placement

152

Position: This study is performed in the supine position.

Active electrode (A): Placement is over the midpoint of the extensor digitorum brevis (EDB) muscle on the dorsum of the foot.

Reference electrode (R): Placement is slightly distal to the 5th metatarsophalangeal joint.

Ground electrode (G): Placement is over the dorsum of the foot.

Stimulation point 1 (S1): The cathode (C) is placed 8 cm proximal to the active electrode, slightly lateral to the tibialis anterior tendon. The anode (A) is proximal.

Stimulation point 2 (S2): The cathode (C) is slightly posterior and inferior to the fibular head. The anode (A) is proximal.

Stimulation point 3 (S3): The cathode (C) is placed approximately 6 to 10 cm proximal to the S2 cathode placement and medial to the tendon of the biceps femoris. The anode (A) is proximal.

F-wave stimulation: The cathode is positioned as for S1, but with the anode distally.

Machine settings: Sensitivity—5 mV/division, Low frequency filter—2 to 3 Hz, High frequency filter—10 kHz, Sweep speed—5 msec/division.

Nerve fibers tested: L5 and S1 nerve roots, through the posterior division of the lumbosacral plexus, and the sciatic and common fibular nerves.

Reference values (1) (242 subjects) (skin temperature over the dorsum of the foot greater than or equal to 31°C):

Onset latency (msec)

Mean	SD	Range	Upper Reference Value
4.8	0.8	3.1–6.9	6.5

Amplitude (mV)

Age Range	Mean	SD	Range	Lower Reference Value
19–39	6.8	2.5	1.6–13	2.6
40–79	5.1	2.5	0.4–11.7	1.1
All subjects	5.9	2.6	0.4–13.8	1.3

Area (mVms)

Age Range	Mean	SD	Range	Lower Reference Value
19–49	20.2	8.0	0.7–39.3	6.8
50–79	14.9	7.6	2.9–37.1	3.6
All subjects	18.3	8.2	0.7–39.3	4.3

Duration (msec)

Mean	SD	Range	Upper Reference Value
5.7	1.0	2.9–9.0	7.7

Nerve conduction velocity (m/sec)

Height in cm (in.)	Age Range	Mean	SD	Range	Lower Reference Value
S1–S2					
<170 cm (<5′7″)	19–39	49	4	42–64	43
	40–79	47	5	38–65	39
≥170 cm (≥5′7″)	19–39	46	4	37–56	37
	40–79	44	4	33–56	36
All subjects		47	4	33–65	38
S2–S3					
All subjects		57	9	38–78	42

F-wave latencies (2) (180 subjects)—shortest of 10 stimuli

Height in cm (in.)	Mean	SD	Range	Upper Reference Value
Age Range 19–39				
<160 (<5′3″)	43.6	2.5	38.5–47.2	48.6
160–169 (5′3″–5′6″)	47.1	3.7	40.8–54.6	54.5
≥170 (≥5′7″)	51.5	4.1	45.6–60.5	59.7
Age Range 40–79				
<160 (<5′3″)	45.4	4.8	39.8–58.1	55.0
160–169 (5′3″–5′6″)	49.6	4.6	44.1–60.0	58.8
≥170 (≥5′7″)	54.6	4.5	45.0–64.2	63.6
All subjects	50.2	5.5	38.5–64.2	61.2

Acceptable Differences

The upper limit of normal increase in latency from one side to the other is 1.6 msec.

The upper limit of normal decrease in amplitude from one side to the other is 61%.

The upper limit of normal decrease in S1 to S2 nerve conduction velocity (NCV) from one side to the other is 8 m/sec.

The upper limit of normal decrease in S2 to S3 NCV from one side to the other is 19 m/sec.

The upper limit of normal decrease in NCV from S1 to S2 and S2 to S3 is 6 m/sec.

The upper limit of normal decrease in amplitude from S1 to S2 is 32%.

The upper limit of normal decrease in amplitude from S2 to S3 is 25%.

The upper limit of normal side-to-side difference in the shortest F-wave latency is 5.1 msec.

The upper limit of normal difference between latencies of the fibular motor to the EDB and the tibial motor to the abductor hallucis in the same limb is 1.8 msec in cases where the fibular nerve has the longer latency; it is 1.5 msec in cases where the tibial nerve latency is longer (3).

Helpful Hints

- Care must be taken at popliteal stimulation to not concomitantly activate the tibial nerve. Moving laterally and distally can help with this. If the waveform is different in shape, or the patient is noted to be plantarflexing during stimulation, then coactivation of the tibial nerve should be suspected.

- An accessory fibular nerve is commonly present (20%–25% incidence), although it is less commonly of clinical significance (4,5). This anomaly can be unilateral or bilateral with partial innervation of the EDB by the accessory deep fibular nerve, a branch of the superficial fibular nerve. This anomaly is inherited in a dominant fashion. The accessory fibular nerve passes behind the lateral malleolus to innervate the EDB. A clue to its existence is when the amplitude obtained by stimulating at the ankle is smaller than at the knee. This is because some of the axons travel in the accessory fibular nerve. In this circumstance, we suggest checking for the accessory fibular nerve by stimulating behind the lateral malleolus and recording over the EDB (9). If a response is recorded from the EDB, an accessory fibular nerve is present.

- A short segment incremental stimulation ("inching") technique has been described for testing the conduction of the fibular nerve portion around the fibular head. The nerve is stimulated in 2 cm increments, starting 4 cm distal, and proceeding to 6 cm proximal to the head of the fibula. In normal subjects, the difference in latency between successive stimulation points varies from 0.2 to 0.7 msec. Abrupt waveform changes or decreases in amplitude may be a sign of conduction block (6,8).

- The compound nerve action potential may be recorded across the fibular head using a technique described by Lee (7). A bar electrode is placed at the very distal portion of the fibular neck. Stimulation is at the medial aspect of the lateral hamstring tendon at the level of the popliteal crease. Sensory settings are used. Normal values were obtained on 70 nerves in 35 normal subjects. The mean amplitude ranged between 23.3 and 24.8 µV, with a standard deviation from 6.9 to 7.4 µV. Mean conduction velocities ranged from 61.6 to 61.7 m/sec, with a standard deviation from 4.3 to 4.5 m/sec.

- The preferred name for this nerve is the fibular nerve (10).

Notes _____

_____

_____

_____

_____

REFERENCES

1. Buschbacher RM. Peroneal nerve motor conduction to the extensor digitorum brevis. *Am J Phys Med Rehabil.* 1999;78:S26–S31.
2. Buschbacher RM. Peroneal F-waves recorded from the extensor digitorum brevis. *Am J Phys Med Rehabil.* 1999;78:S48–S52.
3. Buschbacher RM. Reference values for peroneal nerve motor conduction to the tibialis anterior and for peroneal vs. tibial latencies. *Am J Phys Med Rehabil.* 2003;82(4):296–301.
4. Crutchfield CA, Gutmann L. Hereditary aspects of accessory deep peroneal nerve. *J Neurol Neurosurg Psychiatry.* 1973;36:989–990.
5. Neundoerfer B, Seiberth R. The accessory deep peroneal nerve. *J Neurol.* 1975;209:125–129.
6. Kanakamedala RV, Hong CZ. Peroneal nerve entrapment at the knee localized by short segment stimulation. *Am J Phys Med Rehabil.* 1989;68:116–122.
7. Lee HJ. Compound nerve action potential of common peroneal nerve recorded at fibular neck: its clinical usefulness. *Am J Phys Med Rehabil.* 2001;80:108–112.
8. Raudino F. The value of inching technique in evaluating the peroneal nerve entrapment at the fibular head. *Electrogr Clin Neurophysiol.* 2004;44(1):3–5.
9. Gutmann L. AAEM minimonograph #2: important anomalous innervations of the extremities. *Muscle Nerve.* 1993;16:339–347.
10. Robinson LR. What do we call that structure? *Muscle Nerve.* 2010;42(6):981.

ADDITIONAL READINGS

Falco FJE, Hennessey WJ, Goldberg G, Braddom RL. Standardized nerve conduction studies in the lower limb of the healthy elderly. *Am J Phys Med Rehabil*. 1994;73:168–174.

Lee HJ, Bach JR, DeLisa JA. Peroneal nerve motor conduction to the proximal muscles: an alternative approach to conventional methods. *Am J Phys Med Rehabil*. 1997;76(3):197–199.

Marciniak C, Amon C, Wilson J, Miller R. Practise parameter: utility of electrodiagnostic techniques in evaluating patients with suspected peroneal neuropathy: an evidence based review. *Muscle Nerve*. 2005;31(4):520–527.

FIBULAR MOTOR NERVE TO THE FIBULARIS BREVIS

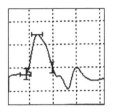

Typical waveform
appearance

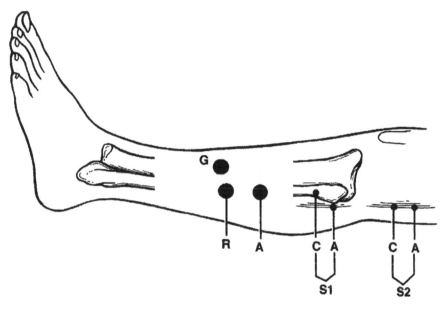

Electrode Placement

Position: This study is performed in the supine position.

Active electrode (A): A 32 mm disc electrode is placed two fifths of the distance from the head of the fibula to the tip of the lateral malleolus.

Reference electrode (R): Placement is distal to the active electrode over the muscle tendon.

Ground electrode (G): Placement is over the tibia, 3 to 4 cm distal to the reference electrode.

Stimulation point 1 (S1): The cathode is placed slightly below the head of the fibula. The anode is proximal.

Stimulation point 2 (S2): The cathode is placed just medial to the lateral border of the popliteal space at the level of the midpatella, approximately 6 to 10 cm proximal to stimulation point 1.

Machine settings: Standard motor settings are used.

Nerve fibers tested: L5, S1, and S2 nerve roots, through the posterior division of the sacral plexus, which become the sciatic nerve and the superficial fibular nerve.

Reference values (1) (34 subjects) (room temperature 22.2–23.3°C):

Onset latency (msec)

Mean	SD	Range	Upper Reference Value
3.0	0.8	1.7–5.4	4.6

Amplitude (mV)

Mean	SD
5.3	1.7

Nerve conduction velocity (m/sec)

Mean	SD	Lower Reference Value
55.3	10.2	35

Helpful Hint

- Calculation of reference values using mean + 2 SD (as done in the cited reference) may produce misleading results when distributions are skewed. Limits of normal noted previously should be interpreted with caution.

Notes

REFERENCE

1. Devi S, Lovelace RE, Duarte N. Proximal peroneal nerve conduction velocity: recording from anterior tibial and peroneus brevis muscles. *Ann Neurol.* 1977;2:116–111.

FIBULAR MOTOR NERVE TO THE FIBULARIS LONGUS

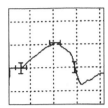

Typical waveform
appearance

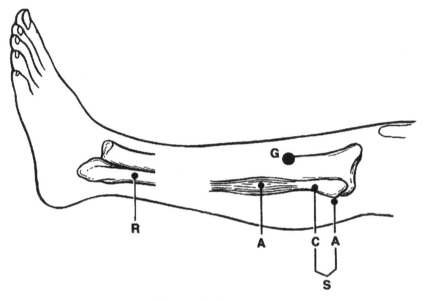

Electrode Placement

Position: This study is performed in the supine position.

Active electrode (A): Placement is 8 cm from the cathode over the fibularis longus on the lateral surface of the fibula.

Reference electrode (R): Placement is at the ankle over the tendon of the fibularis longus muscle.

Ground electrode (G): Placement is over the upper anterior lower leg.

Stimulation point (S): The cathode (C) is placed at the posterolateral aspect of the fibular neck. The anode (A) is proximal.

Machine settings: Sensitivity—2 mV/division (1 mV to determine onset latency), Low frequency filter—2 Hz, High frequency filter—10 kHz, Sweep speed—2 msec/division.

Nerve fibers tested: L5, S1, and S2 nerve roots, through the posterior division of the lumbosacral plexus, the sciatic nerve, and the superficial fibular nerve.

Reference values (1) (81 subjects) (skin temperature over the lateral surface just below the knee joint greater than or equal to 32°C):

Onset latency (msec)

Mean	SD	Range	Upper Reference Value
2.6	0.2	1.9–3.0	3.0

Amplitude (mV)

Mean	SD	Range
6.2	1.7	3.4–10.6

Helpful Hints

- This technique utilizes a fixed distance measurement from a given stimulation site rather than from a given recording site. Therefore, the active electrode is not always over the motor point. This may cause submaximal amplitude measurements to be recorded. It is also not known how accurate the latency measurements are with such a technique. Caution is advised when using such a technique for persons at the extremes of height or high body mass index (BMI).

- The recorded action potential may exhibit multiple peaks, possibly from the volume conducted potentials of adjacent muscles.

Notes

REFERENCE

1. Lee HJ, Bach JR, DeLisa JA. Peroneal nerve motor conduction to the proximal muscles: an alternative approach to conventional methods. *Am J Phys Med Rehabil.* 1997;76:197–199.

FIBULAR MOTOR NERVE TO THE TIBIALIS ANTERIOR

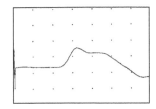

Typical waveform
appearance

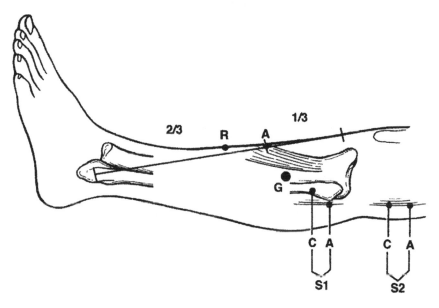

Electrode Placement

Position: This study is performed in the supine position.

Active electrode (A): Placement is one-third of the distance from the tibial tubercle to the lateral malleolus.

Reference electrode (R): Placement is inferomedial to the active electrode, on the bony surface of the tibia.

Ground electrode (G): Placement is between the stimulus and recording electrodes.

Stimulation point 1 (S1): Cathode is placed slightly posterior and inferior to the fibular head, with the anode proximal.

Stimulation point 2 (S2): Approximately 10 cm proximal to the S1 site, slightly medical to the tendon of the biceps femoris. The anode is proximal.

Machine settings: Sensitivity—5 mV/division, Low frequency filter—2 to 3 Hz, High frequency filter—10 kHz, Sweep speed—2 msec/division.

Nerve fibers tested: L4 and L5 nerve roots, through the posterior division of the lumbosacral plexus and the sciatic nerve.

Reference values (1) (244 subjects) (skin temperature over the dorsum of the foot greater than or equal to 31°C):

Onset latency (msec)

Height in cm (in.)	Mean	SD	Range	Upper Reference Value
<160 cm (5′3″)	3.1	0.5	2.2–4.1	4.1
160–180 cm (5′3″–5′11″)	3.5	0.6	2.2–5.2	4.7
>180 cm (5′11″)	4.2	0.6	2.7–5.4	5.4
All subjects	3.6	0.6	2.2–5.4	4.9

Amplitude (mV)

Age Range	Mean	SD	Range	Lower Reference Value
19–29	4.3	1.9	1.3–10.7	2.1
30–79	3.6	1.9	1.1–20.0	1.5
All subjects	3.8	2.0	1.1–20.0	1.7

Area of negative phase (mVms)

Age Range	Mean	SD	Range	Lower Reference Value
19–29	27.4	15.8	4.5–69.6	7.3
30–79	20.2	11.1	4.1–62.1	6.3
All subjects	21.9	12.8	4.1–69.6	6.8

Duration of negative phase (msec)

Mean	SD	Range	Upper Reference Value
10.1	2.5	3.9–15.9	15.0

Nerve conduction velocity (m/sec)

Age Range	Height in cm (in.)	Mean	SD	Range	Lower Reference Value
19–59	<170 (5'7")	66	9	45–87	51
	≥170 (5'7")	59	11	30–89	39
60–79	<170 (5'7")	57	6	47–71	47
	≥170 (5'7")	57	10	37–73	37
All subjects		62	10	30–89	43

Acceptable Differences

The upper limit of normal increase in latency from one side to the other is 1.2 msec.

The upper limit of normal decrease in amplitude from one side to the other is 50%.

The upper limit of normal decrease in NCV from one side to the other is 23 m/sec or 20%.

The upper limit of normal decrease in amplitude between below fibular head stimulation (S1) and above fibular head stimulation (S2) is 36%.

The upper limit of normal difference between tibialis anterior and EDB latency in the same limb is 1.5 msec in cases where the tibialis anterior has the longer latency; it is 1.8 msec in cases where the EDB latency is longer.

Helpful Hints

- Mean NCV across the fibular head was 5 m/sec faster with this study than when recording from the EDB (1,2).

- If a complex waveform is obtained, the reference electrode may be over the muscle. It can be moved distally to the tendon of the tibialis anterior near the ankle, thus moving it further from actively contracting muscle.

Notes _____

_____

_____

_____

_____

_____

_____

_____

REFERENCES

1. Buschbacher RM. Reference values for peroneal nerve motor conduction to the tibialis anterior and for peroneal vs. tibial latencies. *Am J Phys Med Rehabil.* 2003;82:296–301.
2. Buschbacher RM. Peroneal nerve motor conduction to the extensor digitorum brevis. *Am J Phys Med Rehabil.* 1999;78:S26–S31.

ADDITIONAL READINGS

Devi S, Lovelace RE, Duarte N. Proximal peroneal nerve conduction velocity: recording from anterior tibial and peroneus brevis muscles. *Ann Neurol.* 1977;2:116–119.

Lee HJ, Bach JR, DeLisa JA. Peroneal nerve motor conduction to the proximal muscles: an alternative approach to conventional methods. *Am J Phys Med Rehabil.* 1997;76:197–199.

SCIATIC NERVE

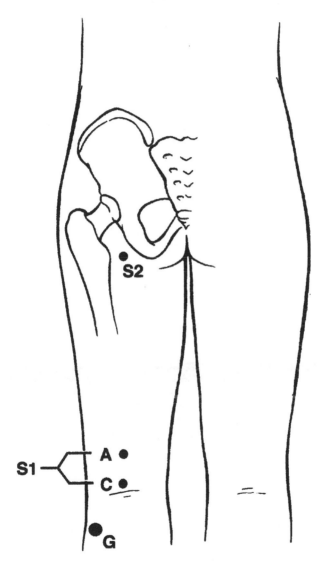

Electrode Placement

Position: This study is performed in the prone position.

Recording electrodes: Placement is on the distal muscles of the foot, such as the EDB (fibular portion), abductor hallucis (tibial portion), or abductor digiti minimi (tibial portion) (see other sections of this book describing recording from these sites: fibular nerve p. 152; tibial nerve p. 178) (1,2).

Ground electrode (G): Placement is between the stimulating and recording electrodes.

Stimulation point 1 (S1): Surface stimulation is applied in the popliteal fossa with the cathode (C) distal and the anode (A) proximal.

Stimulation point 2 (S2): A long needle electrode (cathode) is used to stimulate the sciatic nerve just below the gluteal fold in a line directly above the apex of the popliteal fossa. The anode is placed nearby.

Machine settings: Sensitivity—5 mV/division, Sweep speed—2 msec/division, Low frequency filter—2 to 3 Hz, High frequency filter—10 kHz.

Reference values (1) (18 subjects) (room temperature 23°C–26°C):

Nerve conduction velocity (m/sec)

	Mean	*SD*	*Range*
Tibial portion	52.8	4.7	46.7–59.6
Peroneal portion	54.3	4.4	48.5–61.5

Helpful Hints

- Finding the correct gluteal fold stimulation site may be difficult. The fibular portion of the nerve lies a bit lateral, with the tibial portion being more medial. Observing the foot motion will help identify which portion is being stimulated the most (1).

- With proximal stimulation the recordings made at the EDB may include volume conducted potentials from other foot muscles that are innervated by the tibial portion of the nerve (2).

- Stimulation can also be applied at the ankle to calculate conduction velocity along the leg.

Notes

REFERENCES

1. Ma DM, Liveson JA. *Nerve Conduction Handbook*. Philadelphia, PA: FA Davis; 1983.
2. Yap CB, Hirota T. Sciatic nerve motor conduction velocity study. *J Neurol Neurosurg Psychiatry*. 1967;30:233–239.

ADDITIONAL READINGS/ALTERNATE TECHNIQUES

Alfonsi E, Merlo IM, Clerici AM, et al. Proximal nerve conduction by high-voltage electrical stimulation in S1 radiculopathies and acquired demyelinating neuropathies. *Clin Neurophysiol.* 2003;114(2):239–247.

Gassel MM, Trojaborg W. Clinical and electrophysiological study of the pattern of conduction times in the distribution of the sciatic nerve. *J Neurol Neurosurg Psychiatry.* 1964;27:351–357.

Inaba A, Yokota T, Komori T, Hirose K. Proximal and segmental motor nerve conduction in the sciatic nerve produced by percutaneous high voltage electrical stimulation. *Electroencephalogr Clin Neurophysiol.* 1996;101:100–104.

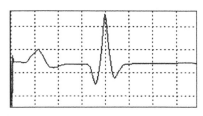

Typical waveform
appearance

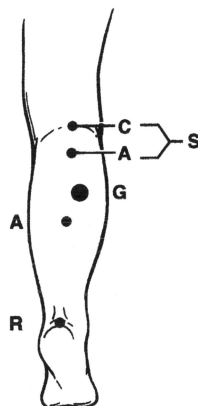

Electrode Placement

Position: This study is performed in the prone position.

Active electrode (A): The subject is placed prone. The knee is passively flexed by the examiner to mark the midpoint of the popliteal crease. The leg is then lowered onto a pillow with the foot hanging over the edge of the table and the ankle slightly plantarflexed. A second mark is placed on the posterior calcaneus. The distance between the two marked points is measured and the active electrode is placed at the midpoint.

Reference electrode (R): Placement is over the posterior calcaneus.

Ground electrode (G): Placement is between the stimulating and recording electrodes.

Stimulation point (S): The cathode (C) is placed at the midpopliteal crease with the anode (A) distal.

Machine settings: Sensitivity—500 µV/division, Low frequency filter—2 to 3 Hz, High frequency filter—10 kHz, Sweep speed—10 msec/division, Stimulus duration—1.0 msec.

Nerve fibers tested: Afferent sciatic nerve fibers, S1 nerve root, monosynaptic spinal cord connection, and efferent sciatic nerve.

Reference values (1) (251 subjects): (skin temperature over the ankle 31°C or greater):

Onset latency (msec)

Height in cm (in.)	Mean	SD	Range	Upper Reference Value
Age Range 19–39				
<160 (<5′3″)	27.1	1.8	23.9–29.8	29.8
160–169 (5′3″–5′6″)	28.6	1.9	21.3–34.1	32.3
170–179 (5′7″–5′10″)	30.3	1.8	26.0–33.7	33.7
⩾180 (⩾5′11″)	32.0	2.1	28.2–35.9	35.9
Age Range 40–49				
<160 (<5′3″)	27.8	1.1	26.4–29.7	29.7
160–169 (5′3″–5′6″)	30.2	1.4	27.2–33.0	32.8
170–179 (5′7″2–5′10″)	31.0	1.6	28.4–33.5	33.5
⩾180 (⩾5′11″)	32.7	2.1	28.2–35.3	33.5
Age Range 50–79				
<160 (<5′3″)	29.3	1.9	2`5.9–35.3	33.6
160–169 (5′3″–5′6″)	31.7	1.6	28.1–35.9	35.6
170–179 (5′7″–5′10″)	31.9	1.7	27.9–35.1	35.6

Height in cm (in.)	Mean	SD	Range	Upper Reference Value
≥180 (≥5'11")	33.2	2.5	29.7–36.4	36.4
All subjects	30.3	2.4	21.3–36.4	35.0

Acceptable Difference

The upper limit of normal increase in latency from one side to the other is 2.0 msec.

Helpful Hints

- Older persons have a higher incidence of unelicitable H-reflexes than do young persons.

- Jankus et al. studied side-to-side amplitude variability for the tibial H-reflex. They included only subjects with side-to-side latency differences of less than 1.5 msec. They concluded that a side-to-side peak-to-peak amplitude ratio smaller than 0.4 in the face of normal latency is probably abnormal (2).

- The H-reflex can be facilitated with slight active plantarflexion.

- The tibial nerve can also be effectively stimulated by placing the anode at the front of the knee, while keeping the cathode as described; this enhances flow of current into deeper structures.

- The peak latencies of the M and H reflex responses can be measured after a single stimulus to the S1 spinal nerve. The normal value is 7 ± 0.3 msec for the interpotential latency difference (central loop) of the H reflex in the S1 spinal nerve in healthy subjects. A central loop latency of greater than 8 msec was correlated with clinical and electromyographic evidence of S1 radiculopathy (3).

Notes

REFERENCES

1. Buschbacher RM. Normal range for H-reflex recording from the calf muscles. *Am J Phys Med Rehabil.* 1999;78:S75–S79.
2. Jankus WR, Robinson LR, Little JW. Normal limits of side to side H-reflex amplitude variability. *Arch Phys Med Rehabil.* 1994;75:3–7.
3. Pease WS, Kozakiewicz R, Johnson EW. Central loop of the H reflex. Normal values and use in S1 radiculopathy. *Am J Phys Med Rehabil.* 1997;76(3):182–184.

ADDITIONAL READINGS

Braddom RL, Johnson EW. Standardization of H reflex and diagnostic use in S1 radiculopathy. *Arch Phys Med Rehabil.* 1974;55:161–166.
Falco FJE, Hennessey WJ, Goldberg G, Braddom RL. H reflex latency in the healthy elderly. *Muscle Nerve.* 1994;17:161–167.

TIBIAL NERVE

TIBIAL MOTOR NERVE (MEDIAL PLANTAR BRANCH) TO THE ABDUCTOR HALLUCIS

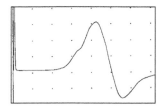

Typical waveform
appearance

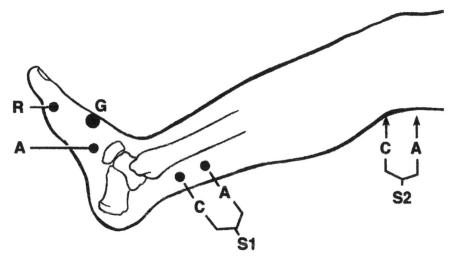

Electrode Placement

Position: This study is performed in the supine position.

Active electrode (A): Placement is over the medial foot, slightly anterior and inferior to the navicular tubercle (at the most superior point of the arch formed by the junction of plantar skin and dorsal foot skin).

Reference electrode (R): Placement is slightly distal to the 1st metatarsophalangeal joint, on the medial surface of the joint.

Ground electrode (G): Placement is over the dorsum of the foot.

Stimulation point 1 (S1): The cathode (C) is placed 8 cm proximal to the active electrode (measured in a straight line with the ankle in neutral position) and slightly posterior to the medial malleolus. The anode (A) is proximal.

Stimulation point 2 (S2): The cathode (C) is placed at the midpopliteal fossa or slightly medial or lateral to the midline. The anode (A) is proximal.

F-wave stimulation: The cathode is positioned as for stimulation point 1, but with the anode distally.

Machine settings: Sensitivity—5 mV/division, Low frequency filter—2 to 3 Hz, High frequency filter—10 kHz, Sweep speed—5 msec/division.

Nerve fibers tested: S1 and S2 nerve roots, through the anterior division of the lumbosacral plexus and the sciatic nerve.

Reference values (1) (250 subjects) (skin temperature over the dorsum of the foot greater than or equal to 31°C):

Onset latency (msec)

Mean	SD	Range	Upper Reference Value
4.5	0.8	3.2–7.4	6.1

Amplitude (mV)

Age Range	Mean	SD	Range	Lower Reference Value
19–29	15.3	4.5	5.3–26.6	5.8
30–59	12.9	4.5	1.8–25.6	5.3
60–79	9.8	4.2	1.0–19.4	1.1
All subjects	12.9	4.8	1.0–26.6	4.4

Area (mVms)

Age Range	Mean	SD	Range	Lower Reference Value
19–49	38.9	14.3	7.1–74.8	14.2
50–79	29.2	13.3	1.8–67.0	5.0
All subjects	35.3	14.7	1.8–74.8	9.1

Duration (msec)

Mean	SD	Range	Upper Reference Value
6.3	1.2	3.7–11.2	8.7

Nerve conduction velocity (m/sec)

Height in cm (in.)	Mean	SD	Range	Lower Reference Value
Age Range 19–49				
<160 (<5′3″)	51	4	44–59	44
160–169 (5′3″–5′6″)	49	6	39–77	42
≥170 (≥5′7″)	47	5	36–67	37
Age Range 50–79				
<160 (<5′3″)	49	5	40–62	40
160–169 (5′3″–5′6″)	45	5	37–56	37
≥170 (≥5′7″)	44	5	34–52	34
All subjects	47	6	34–77	39

F-wave latencies (msec) (2) (180 subjects)—shortest of 10 stimuli

Height in cm (in.)	Mean	SD	Range	Upper Reference Value
Age Range 19–39				
<160 (<5′3″)	43.2	2.2	39.1–45.4	47.6
160–169 (5′3″–5′6″)	47.2	3.0	41.9–52.7	53.2
170–179 (5′7″–5′10″)	52.0	4.0	45.6–59.2	60.0
≥180 (≥5′11″)	53.1	4.4	47.0–59.8	61.9
Age Range 40–79				
<160 (<5′3″)	46.8	4.6	38.5–57.2	56.0
160–169 (5′3″–5′6″)	50.5	3.5	44.8–59.7	57.5
170–179 (5′7″–5′10″)	53.9	3.6	45.1–59.0	61.1
≥180 (≥5′11″)	57.9	5.3	52.0–767.0	68.5
All subjects	50.8	5.3	38.5–67.0	61.4

Acceptable Differences

The upper limit of normal increase in latency from one side to the other is 1.4 msec.

The upper limit of normal decrease in amplitude from one side to the other is 50%.

The upper limit of normal decrease in NCV from one side to the other is 10 m/sec.

The upper limit of normal decrease in amplitude from ankle to knee stimulation is 71%.

The upper limit of normal side-to-side difference in the shortest F-wave latency is 5.7 msec.

Helpful Hints

- Ankle stimulation should be approximately halfway between the medial malleolus and the Achilles tendon.

- Care should be taken to not concomitantly stimulate the fibular nerve at the knee. Stimulation should be close to the midline of the popliteal fossa, but the stimulator may need to be moved slightly medially or laterally to obtain an optimal response. Watching for the direction of foot motion on stimulation will help ensure that the proper nerve is stimulated.

- Obtaining a similar size response at knee and ankle stimulation may be difficult at times. The amplitude drop with knee versus ankle stimulation for this nerve study is greater than that seen with most other nerve studies, due to electrical activity seen at the reference electrode, which creates phase cancellation with the active electrode.

- In subjects with large feet, the 8 cm fixed distance between stimulating and recording electrodes may fail to include the entire "tarsal tunnel" area. A 10 cm distance can be used (3,4). With the active electrode 1 cm posterior and inferior to the navicular tubercle and a 10 cm distance between the stimulating and recording electrodes, the mean latency has been described as 3.8 ± 0.5 msec (at 29°C–34°C) (3). In a series of elderly subjects using slightly different methodology from the data presented, the mean latency at 10 cm (again recording posterior and inferior to the navicular tubercle) was 4.5 ± 0.7 msec (4).

- When performing F-wave measurements, an A-wave can often (about 20% of the time) be observed in the tibial nerve.

Notes _____

_____

_____

_____

_____

_____

_____

_____

_____

_____

_____

_____

_____

_____

_____

_____

_____

_____

_____

REFERENCES

1. Buschbacher RM. Tibial nerve motor conduction to the abductor hallucis. *Am J Phys Med Rehabil*. 1999;78:S15–S20.
2. Buschbacher RM. Tibial nerve F-waves recorded from the abductor hallucis. *Am J Phys Rehabil*. 1999;78:S42–S47.

3. Fu R, DeLisa JA, Kraft GH. Motor nerve latencies through the tarsal tunnel in normal adult subjects: standard determinations corrected for temperature and distance. *Arch Phys Med Rehabil*. 1980;61:243–248.
4. Falco FJE, Hennessey WJ, Goldberg G, Braddom RL. Standardized nerve conduction studies in the lower limb of the healthy elderly. *Am J Phys Med Rehabil*. 1994;73:168–174.

ADDITIONAL READINGS

Felsenthal G, Bulter DH, Shear MS. Across-tarsal-tunnel motor-nerve conduction technique. *Arch Phys Med Rehabil*. 1992;73:64–69.

Irani KD, Grabois M, Harvey SC. Standardized technique for diagnosis of tarsal tunnel syndrome. *Am J Phys Med Rehabil*. 1982;61:26–31.

TIBIAL MOTOR NERVE (LATERAL PLANTAR BRANCH) TO THE FLEXOR DIGITI MINIMI BREVIS

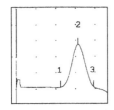

Typical waveform appearance

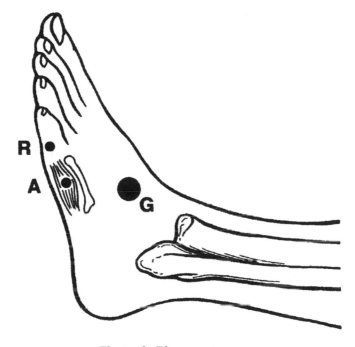

Electrode Placement

Position: This study is performed in the supine position.

Active electrode (A): Placement is on the midpoint of the inferolateral edge of the 5th metatarsal.

Reference electrode (R): Placement is slightly distal to the 5th metatarsophalangeal joint on the lateral surface of the joint.

Ground electrode (G): Placement is on the dorsum of the foot.

Stimulation point (S): Stimulation is applied at the same point as for the study recording from the abductor hallucis (see section on the tibial motor nerve study to the abductor hallucis, p. 178). The cathode (C) is placed behind the medial malleolus 8 cm proximal to a point slightly anterior and inferior to the navicular tubercle on the medial foot. The anode (A) is proximal.

Machine settings: Sensitivity—5 mV/division, Low frequency filter—2 to 3 Hz, High frequency filter—10 kHz, Sweep speed—5 msec/division.

Nerve fibers tested: S1 and S2 nerve roots, through the anterior division of the lumbosacral plexus and the sciatic nerve.

Reference values (1) (205 subjects) (skin temperature over the dorsum of the foot at least 31°C):

Onset latency (msec)

Mean	SD	Range	Upper Reference Value
6.4	1.0	2.8–11.0	8.3

Amplitude (mV)

Age Range	Mean	SD	Range	Lower Reference Value
19–29	7.8	3.2	2.5–16.9	2.8
30–59	6.0	3.2	1.2–15.9	1.7
60–79	4.7	3.1	1.0–15.1	1.0
All subjects	6.1	3.3	1.0–16.9	1.4

Area (mVms)

Age Range	Mean	SD	Range	Lower Reference Value
19–59	17.5	9.5	1.8–48.7	4.2
60–79	11.8	6.6	1.0–26.8	3.1
All subjects	16.2	9.2	1.0–48.7	3.1

Duration (msec)

Mean	SD	Range	Upper Reference Value
5.8	1.7	2.1–11.9	10.0

Acceptable Differences

The upper limit of normal increase in latency from one side to the other is 1.5 msec.

The upper limit of normal decrease in amplitude from one side to the other is 58%.

Normally, the lateral branch latency is greater than the medial branch latency. The upper limit of normal increase in latency to the flexor digiti minimi brevis versus the abductor hallucis is 3.5 msec. If the medial latency comes within 0.3 msec of the lateral latency or exceeds the lateral latency, this is a sign of medial branch slowing.

Helpful Hints

- This study is very easy to perform and allows comparison of the lateral plantar nerve to the medial plantar nerve.

- Previous authors have used this same recording site but have remarked that the recording is from the abductor digiti minimi. Recent research has identified the source of this potential to be coming from the flexor digiti minimi brevis (2).

Notes

REFERENCES

1. Buschbacher RM. Tibial motor conduction to the flexor digiti minimi brevis. *Am J Phys Med Rehabil.* 1999;78:S21–S25.
2. Del Toro DR, Mazur A, Dwzierzynski WW, Park TA. Electrophysiologic mapping and cadaveric dissection of the lateral floor: implications for tibial motor nerve conduction studies. *Arch Phys Med Rehabil.* 1998;78:823–826.

ADDITIONAL READINGS

Felsenthal G, Bulter DH, Shear MS. Across-tarsal-tunnel motor-nerve conduction technique. *Arch Phys Med Rehabil.* 1992;73:64–69.
Irani KD, Grabois M, Harvey SC. Standardized technique for diagnosis of tarsal tunnel syndrome. *Am J Phys Med Rehabil.* 1982;61:26–31.
Patel AT, Gaines K, Malamut R, et al. American Association of Neuromuscular and Electrodiagnostic Medicine. Usefulness of electrodiagnostic techniques in the evaluation of suspected tarsal tunnel syndrome: an evidence based review. *Muscle Nerve.* 2005;32(2):236–240.

CHAPTER 4

LOWER LIMB SENSORY AND MIXED NERVE STUDIES

Typical waveform
appearance

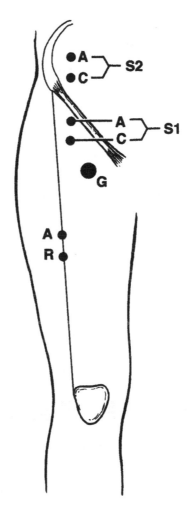

Electrode Placement—Ma and Liveson Technique

Ma and Liveson Technique

Position: This study is performed in the supine position.

Recording electrodes: Surface electrodes are placed along a line connecting the anterior superior iliac spine (ASIS) to the lateral border of the patella, with the active electrode (A) 17–20 cm distal to the ASIS and the reference electrode (R) 3 cm more distal.

Ground electrode (G): Placement is between the stimulating and recording electrodes.

Stimulation point 1 (S1): Stimulation can be applied below the inguinal ligament over the origin of the sartorius.

Stimulation point 2 (S2): Stimulation can be applied above the inguinal ligament 1 cm medial to the ASIS.

Machine settings: Sensitivity—5 µV/division, Low frequency filter—32 Hz, High frequency filter—3.2 kHz.

Nerve fibers tested: L2 and L3 nerve roots through the posterior division of the lumbosacral plexus.

Reference values (1) (20 subjects) (room temperature 23°C–26°C):

Onset latency (msec)

	Mean	SD	Range
S1 (14–18 cm)	2.5	0.2	2.2–2.8
S2 (17–20 cm)	2.8	0.4	2.3–3.2

Peak-to-peak amplitude (µV)

	Mean	SD	Range
S1	7.0	1.8	4–11
S2	6.0	1.5	3–10

Helpful Hints

- This study is technically difficult, especially in overweight persons. Absent responses are of questionable clinical significance.

- For S2 stimulation it may help to exert pressure toward the ASIS. Rotating the anode may be necessary to reduce stimulus artifact.

- Care should be used when using mean ±2 SD to establish reference values, as the data may not follow a normal distribution and misleading limits may be derived.

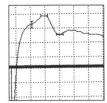

Typical waveform
appearance

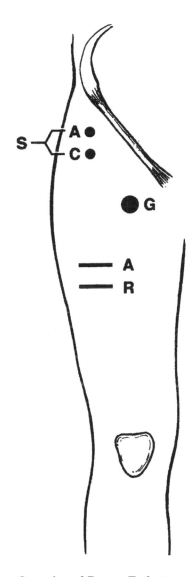

Electrode Placement—Spevak and Prevec Technique

Spevak and Prevec Technique

Position: This study is performed in the supine position.

Recording electrodes: Two 8 cm long strip electrodes are placed 2.5 cm apart (A and R) on the anterolateral thigh, approximately 25 cm distal to the stimulating electrode.

Ground electrode (G): Placement is between the stimulating and recording electrodes.

Stimulation point (S): Stimulation is applied 6–10 cm below the ASIS. The point where a sensation radiates to the lateral thigh is sought. Stimulus duration is 0.1 msec with the intensity set to double the sensory threshold and not above 150 V. Eight to 32 responses are averaged.

Machine settings: Sensitivity—1–2 µV/division, Low frequency filter—100 Hz, High frequency filter—5 kHz, Sweep speed—1 msec/division.

Reference values (2) (29 subjects—distance 25.3 ± 3.5 cm) (skin temperature over the thigh 29°C–32.5°C):

Onset latency (msec)

Mean	SD	Upper Reference Value
4.1	0.7	5.5

Peak latency (msec)

Mean	SD	Upper Reference Value
4.6	0.7	6.0

Nerve conduction velocity (m/sec) calculated for onset latency

Mean	SD	Lower Reference Value
62.3	5.5	51.3

Peak-to-peak amplitude (µV)

Mean	SD
2.0	1.0

Duration (msec)

Mean	SD	Upper Reference Value
1.9	0.5	2.9

Acceptable Differences

The side-to-side difference in conduction velocity is 2.6 ± 2.2 m/sec and never exceeded 6 m/sec in the cited study.

The side-to-side difference in amplitude is 0.86 ± 0.89 µV.

Helpful Hints

- If the response is unobtainable, it is of doubtful clinical significance. If present, slowing of conduction velocity or a greater than normal side-to-side conduction velocity difference are most sensitive to pathology.

- This study will be normal in cases of purely local slowing across the inguinal ligament segment.

- The use of ultrasound guidance for surface electrode placement can improve the likelihood of obtaining a response and reduce side-to-side variability in responses obtained. The use of ultrasound guided near nerve needle recording for lateral femoral cutaneous sensory nerves improves the response amplitude significantly. We recommend that for patients with a body mass index (BMI) >27.5, ultrasound guidance be utilized.

- Care should be used when using mean ±2 SD to establish reference values, as the data may not follow a normal distribution and misleading limits may be derived.

Notes

REFERENCES

1. Ma DM, Liveson JA. *Nerve Conduction Handbook.* Philadelphia, PA: FA Davis; 1983.
2. Spevak MK, Prevec TS. A noninvasive method of neurography in meralgia paresthetica. *Muscle Nerve.* 1995;18:601–605.

ADDITIONAL READINGS/ALTERNATE TECHNIQUES

Boon AJ, Bailey PW, Smith J, et al. Utility of ultrasound guided surface electrode placement in lateral femroal cutaneous nerve conduction studies. *Muscle Nerve.* 2011;44(4):525–530.

Deimel GW, Hurst RW, Sorenson EJ, Boon AJ. Utility of ultrasound guided near nerve needle recording for lateral femoral cutaneous sensory nerve study: does it increase reliability compared to surface recording? *Muscle Nerve.* 2013;47(2):274–276.

Karandreas N, Papatheodorou A, Triantaphilos I, et al. Sensory nerve conduction studies of the less frequently examined nerves. *Electromyogr Clin Neurophysiol.* 1995;35:169–173.

Lysens R, Vandendriessche G, VanMol Y, Rosselle N. The sensory conduction velocity in the cutaneous femoris lateralis nerve in normal adult subjects and in patients with complaints suggesting meralgia paresthetica. *Electromyogr Clin Neurophysiol.* 1981;21:505–510.

Shin YB, Park JH, Kwon DR, Park BK. Variability in conduction of the lateral femoral cutaneous nerve. *Muscle Nerve.* 2006;33(5):645–649.

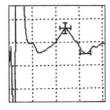

Typical waveform
appearance

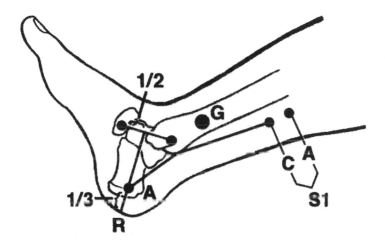

Electrode Placement

Position: This study is performed in the supine position.

Active electrode (A): Placement is one-third of the distance from the apex of the heel to a point midway between the navicular tubercle and the prominence of the medial malleolus.

Reference electrode (R): Placement is over the apex of the heel.

Ground electrode (G): Placement is between the stimulating and recording electrodes.

Stimulation point (S): The cathode (C) is placed 10 cm proximal to the active electrode, measuring first to the posterior tip of the medial malleolus and then along the medial border of the tibia. The cathode is placed 1–2 cm posterior to the medial edge of the tibia. The anode (A) is proximal or rotated to minimize stimulus artifact.

Machine settings: Sensitivity—10–20 µV/division, Low frequency filter—2 Hz, High frequency filter—2 kHz, Sweep speed—1 msec/division.

Nerve fibers tested: S1 nerve root through the anterior division of the lumbosacral plexus and the tibial nerve.

Reference values (1) (36 subjects) (skin temperature greater than or equal to 31°C):

Onset latency (msec)

Mean	SD	Range	Upper Reference Value
1.7	0.3	1.4–2.0	2.0

Peak latency (msec)

Mean	SD	Range	Upper Reference Value
2.5	0.3	2.2–2.8	2.8

Baseline-to-peak amplitude (µV)

Mean	Range	Lower Reference Value
18	8–34	8

Acceptable Differences

The upper limit of normal side-to-side difference in onset latency is 0.3 msec. The upper limit of normal side-to-side difference in peak latency is 0.3 msec. The upper limit of normal side-to-side difference in amplitude is 12 µV.

Helpful Hints

- This sensory response may need to be averaged.

- The sensory response is often followed by volume conducted motor artifact.

- Proper skin preparation is recommended consisting of: preparing the active and reference electrode sites with abrasive tape and cleaning the skin with alcohol.

Notes

REFERENCE

1. Park TA, DelToro DR. The medial calcaneal nerve: anatomy and nerve conduction technique. *Muscle Nerve*. 1995;18:32–38.

MEDIAL FEMORAL CUTANEOUS SENSORY NERVE

Typical waveform
appearance

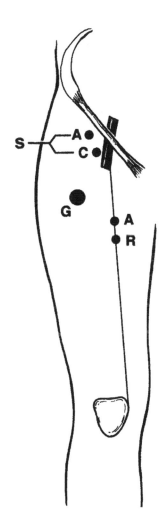

Electrode Placement

Position: This study is performed in the supine position.

Active electrode (A): The active electrode is placed 14 cm distal to the femoral pulse in the inguinal area, along an imaginary line from the pulse to the medial border of the patella.

Reference electrode (R): The reference electrode is placed 4 cm distal to the active electrode on this same imaginary line.

Ground electrode (G): Placement is proximal to the active electrode on the lateral thigh.

Stimulation point (S): The cathode (C) is placed immediately lateral to the femoral artery in the inguinal area. The anode (A) is proximal.

Machine settings: Sensitivity—5 µV/division, Low frequency filter—20 Hz, High frequency filter—2 kHz, Sweep speed—1 msec/division, Stimulator pulse duration—0.2 msec.

Nerve fibers tested: L2 and L3 nerve roots through the posterior division of the lumbosacral plexus and the femoral nerve.

Reference values (1) (32 subjects) (temperature over the midmedial thigh of 33°C or more):

Onset latency (msec)

Mean	SD	Range	Upper Reference Value
2.3–2.4	0.2	1.9–2.9	2.7–2.8

Peak latency (msec)

Mean	SD	Range	Upper Reference Value
2.9	0.2–0.3	2.3–3.5	3.3–3.5

Onset-to-peak amplitude (µV)

Mean	SD	Range
4.8–4.9	1.0	3.4–7.9

Helpful Hints

- Averaging of approximately 5 to 10 recordings is often necessary.

- Anode rotation is often required to reduce stimulus artifact.

- The stimulating electrodes may need to be moved medially or laterally to obtain a recording.

- The leg should be relaxed with the knee slightly flexed. It may be useful to support the knee with a pillow.

Notes

REFERENCE

1. Lee HJ, Bach JR, DeLisa JA. Medial femoral cutaneous nerve conduction. *Am J Phys Med Rehabil.* 1995;74:305–307.

FIBULAR NERVE

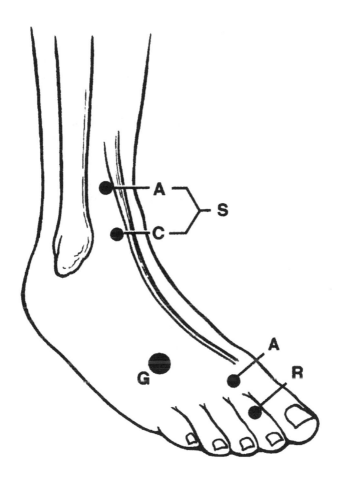

Electrode Placement

Position: This study is performed in the supine position.

Active electrode (A): Placement is over the terminal sensory branch of the nerve at the interspace between the 1st and 2nd metatarsal heads.

Reference electrode (R): Placement is 3 cm distal to the active electrode on the 2nd digit.

Ground electrode (G): Placement is between the stimulating and recording electrodes on the dorsum of the foot.

Stimulation point (S): The cathode (C) is placed at the ankle, 12 cm proximal to the active electrode and just lateral to the extensor hallucis longus tendon. The anode (A) is proximal.

Machine settings: Electronic averaging is used (5–20 stimuli). Sensitivity—5 µV/ division, Low frequency filter—20 Hz, High frequency filter—2 kHz, Sweep speed—1 msec/division.

Nerve fibers tested: L5 nerve root, through the posterior division of the lumbosacral plexus and the common and deep peroneal nerves.

Normal values (1) (40 subjects) (skin temperature over the dorsum of the foot greater than or equal to 29°C):

Onset latency (msec)

Mean	SD	Range
2.9	0.4	2.1–3.6

Peak latency (msec)

Mean	SD	Range
3.6	0.4	2.7–4.2

Onset-to-peak amplitude (µV)

Mean	SD	Range
3.4	1.2	1.6–6.6

Notes _____

_____

_____

_____

_____

_____

_____

_____

_____

_____

_____

_____

_____

_____

_____

_____

REFERENCE

1. Lee HJ, Bach JR, DeLisa JA. Deep peroneal sensory nerve: standardization in nerve conduction study. *Am J Phys Med Rehabil*. 1990;69:202–204.

ADDITIONAL READINGS/ALTERNATE TECHNIQUES

Lo YL, Leoh TH, Dan YF, et al. An electrophysiological study of the deep peroneal sensory nerve. *Eur Neurol*. 2003;50:244–247.

Ponsford S. Medial (cutaneous) branch of deep common peroneal nerve: recording technique and a case report. *Electroencephalogr Clin Neurophysiol.* 1994;93:159–160.

Posas HN Jr, Rivner MH. Nerve conduction studies of the medial branch of the deep peroneal nerve. *Muscle Nerve.* 1990;13:862.

Weimer LH, Trojaborg W, Marquinez AI, et al. The deep peroneal sensory nerve: a reliable source of nerve conduction data? Presented at the AAEM Annual Meeting; October 17, 1998; Orlando, FL.

SUPERFICIAL FIBULAR SENSORY NERVE (INTERMEDIATE DORSAL CUTANEOUS BRANCH)

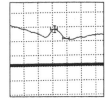

Typical waveform
appearance

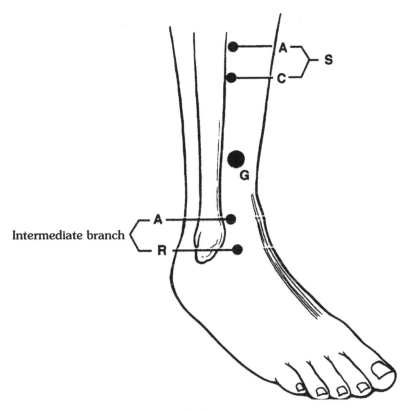

Electrode Placement

Izzo et al. Technique

Position: This study is performed in the supine position.

Active electrodes (A): Placement is at the level of the ankle after localization by inspection and palpation during plantar flexion and inversion (the nerve can usually be easily identified in this position).

Reference electrode (R): Placement is 3–4 cm distal to the active electrode for both branches (1,2).

Ground electrode (G): Placement is over the distal dorsal lower leg, between the active electrodes and the cathode.

Stimulation point (S): The cathode (C) is placed 14 cm proximal to the active electrode on the anterolateral aspect of the leg. The anode (A) is proximal.

Machine settings: Sensitivity—20 µV/division, Low frequency filter—20 Hz, High frequency filter—2 kHz, Sweep speed—2 msec/division.

Nerve fibers tested: L4, L5, and S1 nerve roots, through the posterior division of the lumbosacral plexus and the common fibular nerve.

Reference values (1) (80 subjects) (ankle skin temperature of at least 28°C):

Onset latency (msec)

Intermediate Branch

Mean	SD	Range	Upper Reference Value
2.8	0.3	2.2–3.6	3.4

Peak latency (msec)

Intermediate Branch

Mean	SD	Range	Upper Reference Value
3.4	0.4	2.8–4.6	4.2

Peak-to-peak amplitude (μV)

Intermediate Branch

Mean	SD	Range
15.1	8.2	4–40

Data for 122 elderly subjects (unobtainable in 12), aged 60–89 years, mean 74.1, with skin temperature over the extensor digitorum brevis at least 29°C (2).

Helpful Hints

- These nerve branches are superficial and can often be palpated or seen passing under the surface of the skin, especially when the foot is plantarflexed and inverted (1).

- A stimulus duration of 0.05–0.1 msec was used to derive the data presented by Izzo and colleagues (1).

- In approximately 2% of subjects a response is unobtainable from the intermediate branch (1).

Jabre Technique (Intermediate Branch)

Recording electrodes: A bar electrode is placed at the level of the lateral malleolus, one to two fingerbreadths medial to the malleolus. The active electrode (A) is proximal and the reference electrode (R) is distal (3,4).

Ground electrode (G): The ground electrode is placed over the anterior lower leg, between the stimulating and recording electrodes.

Stimulation point (S): The cathode (C) is placed 12 cm proximal to the active electrode with the stimulator probe held firmly against the anterior aspect of the fibula. The anode (A) is proximal.

Machine settings: Sensitivity—10 μV/division, Low frequency filter—32 Hz, High frequency filter—1.6 kHz, Sweep speed—2 msec/division.

Normal values (3) (36 subjects) (data derived at an ambient temperature of 70°F, 21°C):

Peak latency (msec)

Mean	SD	Upper Reference Value
2.9	0.3	3.5

Onset-to-negative peak amplitude (μV)

Mean	SD
20.5	6.1

Helpful Hints

- In some cases, the nerve can be palpated for easier localization.

- A relatively low stimulus intensity may be necessary to avoid contamination by motor artifact.

- The data reported here were derived using a 0.05 msec pulse duration. A 0.1 msec pulse duration may be required in some cases.

- A second, more proximal stimulation allows for calculation of a conduction velocity. Stimulation is applied 8–9 cm proximal to the previously-described stimulation point. The conduction velocity of 17 subjects was 65.7 ± 3.7 m/sec between these points (3).

- Kushnir et al. (5) studied 52 patients with clinical evidence of mild chronic sensorimotor polyneuropathy and normal sural nerve responses and found that the superficial fibular nerve was abnormal with regards to amplitude and conduction velocity. One should consider superficial fibular sensory nerve testing in the routine electrodiagnostic evaluation of patients with suspected polyneuropathy and normal sural nerve responses. The use of the superficial fibular nerve improves the detection rate of peripheral neuropathy (6).

Notes _____

_____

_____

_____

_____

_____

REFERENCES

1. Izzo KL, Sridhara CR, Rosenholtz H, Lemont H. Sensory conduction studies of the branches of the superficial peroneal nerve. *Arch Phys Med Rehabil.* 1981;62:24–27.

2. Falco FJE, Hennessey WJ, Goldberg G, Braddom RL. Standardized nerve conduction studies in the lower limb of the healthy elderly. *Am J Phys Med Rehabil.* 1994;73:168–174.

3. Jabre JF. The superficial peroneal sensory nerve revisited. *Arch Neurol.* 1981;38:666–667.

4. Jabre JF, Hackett ER. *EMG Manual.* Springfield, IL: Charles C. Thomas; 1983.

5. Kushnir M, Klein C, Kimiagar Y, et al. Medial dorsal superficial peroneal nerve studies in patients with polyneuropathy and normal sural responses. *Muscle Nerve.* 2005;31:386–389.

6. Lo Yl, Xu LQ, Leoh TH, et al. Superficial peroneal sensory and sural nerve conduction studies in peripheral neuropathy. *J Clin Neurosci.* 2006;13(5):547–549.

ADDITIONAL READINGS/ALTERNATE TECHNIQUES

Karandreas N, Papatheodorou A, Triantaphilos I, et al. Sensory nerve conduction studies of the less frequently examined nerves. *Electromyogr Clin Neurophysiol.* 1995;35:169–173.

Takahashi N, Takahashi O, Takahashi M, et al. A new method of superficial peroneal nerve conduction studies. *Electromyogr Clin Neuophysiol.* 2003;43:507–510.

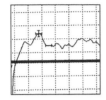

Typical waveform
appearance

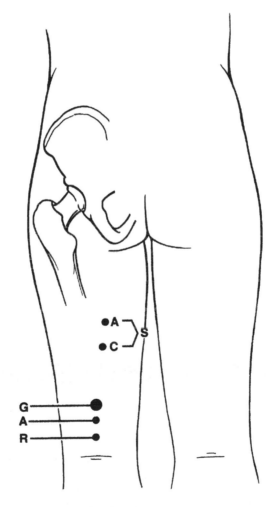

Electrode Placement

Position: This study is performed in the prone position.

Recording electrodes: A bar electrode is placed at the midline of the posterior thigh, with the active electrode (A) 6 cm proximal to the midpopliteal region. The reference (R) electrode is distal.

Ground electrode (G): Placement is just proximal to the bar electrode.

Stimulation point (S): The cathode (C) is placed 12 cm proximal to the active electrode on a line connecting the active electrode with the ischial tuberosity, in the groove between the medial and lateral hamstring musculature (the intermuscular groove can be palpated by having the subject flex the knee). The anode (A) is proximal.

Machine settings: Sensitivity—5 µV/division, Low frequency filter—20 Hz, High frequency filter—2 kHz, Sweep speed—1–2 msec/division.

Nerve fibers tested: Posterior divisions of the S1 and S2 nerve roots and anterior divisions of the S2 and S3 nerve roots.

Reference values (1) (40 subjects) (skin temperature of the posterior thigh maintained between 32°C and 33°C):

Peak latency (msec)

Mean	SD	Range	Upper Reference Value
2.8	0.2	2.3–3.3	3.2

Peak-to-peak amplitude (µV)

Mean	SD	Range
6.5	1.5	4.1–12.0

Helpful Hints

- Local depolarization of the surrounding musculature may occur on stimulation. This does not generally obscure the sensory waveform but is a theoretical confounding factor.

- Study of the posterior femoral cutaneous nerve may facilitate the proximal evaluation of lower extremity peripheral neuropathies, lesions of the posterior femoral cutaneous nerve, or the assessment of the peripheral nervous system in persons with lower extremity amputations.

Notes

REFERENCE

1. Dumitru D, Nelson MR. Posterior femoral cutaneous nerve conduction. *Arch Phys Med Rehabil.* 1990;71:979–982.

SAPHENOUS NERVE

SAPHENOUS SENSORY NERVE (DISTAL TECHNIQUE)

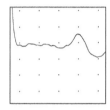

Typical waveform
appearance

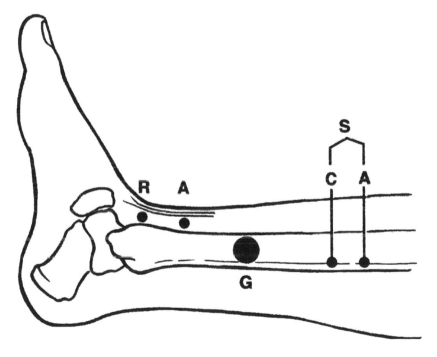

Electrode Placement

Position: This study is performed in the supine position.

Recording electrodes: A 3 cm bar electrode is used. The reference electrode (R) is positioned slightly anterior to the highest prominence of the medial malleolus, between the malleolus and the tendon of the tibialis anterior. The active electrode (A) is proximal and slightly medial to the tibialis anterior tendon.

Ground electrode (G): Placement is between the recording electrodes and the cathode.

Stimulation point (S): The cathode (C) is placed 14 cm proximal to the active electrode deep to the medial border of the tibia. The anode (A) is proximal.

Machine settings: Sensitivity—2–5 µV/division, Low frequency filter—20 Hz, High frequency filter—2 kHz, Sweep speed—1 msec/division.

Nerve fibers tested: L3 and L4 nerve roots, through the posterior division of the lumbosacral plexus. This nerve is a continuation of the femoral nerve.

Reference values (1) (230 subjects) (skin temperature over the dorsum of the foot greater than or equal to 32°C):

Onset latency (msec)

Mean	SD	Range	Upper Reference Value
3.2	0.3	2.1–3.9	3.8

Peak latency (msec)

Mean	SD	Range	Upper Reference Value
3.8	0.3	2.3–4.6	4.4

Onset-to-peak amplitude (µV)

Mean	SD	Range	Lower Reference Value
6	3	1–15	2

Peak-to-peak amplitude (µV)

Mean	SD	Range	Lower Reference Value
5	4	1–24	1

Area under the curve from onset to positive peak (μVms)

Mean	SD	Range	Lower Reference Value
4	3	1–16	1

Duration (msec)

Mean	SD	Range	Upper Reference Value
1.3	0.3	0.4–2.3	1.9

Acceptable Differences

The upper limit of normal increase in onset and peak latency from one side to the other is 0.5 msec.

The upper limit of normal decrease in onset-to-peak amplitude from one side to the other is 65%.

The upper limit of normal decrease in peak-to-peak amplitude from one side to the other is 78%.

The upper limit of normal difference between sural and saphenous onset latency in the same limb is 0.3 msec in cases where the sural has the longer latency; it is 0.7 msec in cases where the saphenous latency is longer.

The upper limit of normal difference between sural and saphenous peak latency in the same limb is 0.5 msec in cases where the sural has the longer latency; it is 0.6 msec in cases where the saphenous latency is longer.

Helpful Hints

- Small amplitudes are common.

- Firm pressure should be applied to the stimulator. The plantar flexors should be relaxed and the ankle can be placed in slight plantarflexion (2).

- Averaging may be necessary.

- This response is often unrecordable; thus, absent responses are not necessarily pathologic.

- A sweep speed of 5 msec/division has been described to improve visualization of the waveform with low amplitude potentials (2).

Notes

_____

_____

_____

_____

_____

_____

_____

_____

_____

REFERENCES

1. Buschbacher RM. Sural and saphenous 14-cm antidromic sensory nerve conduction studies. *Am J Phys Med Rehabil.* 2003;82(6):421–426.
2. Wainapel SF, Kim DJ, Ebel A. Conduction studies of the saphenous nerve in healthy subjects. *Arch Phys Med Rehabil.* 1978;59:316–319.

ADDITIONAL READING

Izzo KL, Sridhara CR, Rosenholtz H, Lemont H. Sensory conduction studies of the branches of the superficial peroneal nerve. *Arch Phys Med Rehabil.* 1981;62:24–27.

SAPHENOUS SENSORY NERVE (PROXIMAL TECHNIQUE)

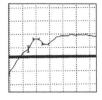

Typical waveform
appearance

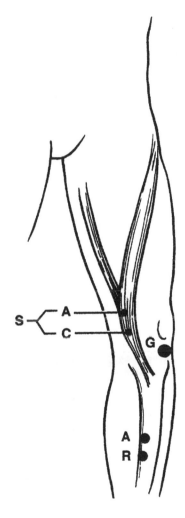

Electrode Placement

Position: This study is performed in the supine position.

Recording electrodes: The active electrode (A) is placed 15 cm distal to the cathode on the medial border of the tibia. The reference electrode (R) is placed 3 cm distally. A 3 cm bar electrode can be used.

Ground electrode (G): Placement is between the stimulating and recording electrodes.

Stimulation point (S): The knee is slightly flexed. The cathode (C) is placed on the medial knee between the tendons of the sartorius and gracilis muscles, approximately 1 cm above the level of the inferior border of the patella. The anode (A) is proximal.

Machine settings: Sensory settings are used.

Nerve fibers tested: L3 and L4 nerve roots, through the posterior division of the lumbosacral plexus. This nerve is a continuation of the femoral nerve.

Reference values (1) (28 subjects—over a 13–16 cm distance) (room temperature 23°C–26°C):

Onset latency (msec)

Mean	SD	Range
2.5	0.19	2.2–2.8

Peak-to-peak amplitude (μV)

Mean	SD	Range
10.23	2.05	7.0–15.0

Helpful Hints

- This nerve may be difficult to localize, especially in obese persons. The hamstring tendon can be palpated at the posterior aspect of the medial knee. Anterior to this is the gracilis, then the sartorius.

- If stimulation is performed too far anteriorly, subjects may report a sensation in the patellar region. They should feel paresthesias in the medial foreleg to the ankle.

- Firm pressure should be applied to the stimulating and recording electrodes.

- Care should be used when using mean ±2 SD to establish reference values, as the data may not follow a normal distribution and misleading limits may be derived.

- A study of the infrapatellar branch of the saphenous nerve has also been described (2). Twenty-five subjects were tested using an active electrode at the inferior medial edge of the patella with the reference electrode on the lower edge of the patella. Stimulation was applied just superior to the medial epicondyle of the femur between the sartorius and gracilis muscles. Onset latency was 1.56 ± 0.3 msec. Peak latency was 1.9 ± 0.2 msec. Baseline-to-peak amplitude was 4 ± 2.1 µV. Maximum side-to-side difference was 0.4 msec for latency and 3.7 µV for amplitude. A response was obtained in 90% of subjects after averaging 20 recordings.

Notes

REFERENCES

1. Ma DM, Liveson JA. *Nerve Conduction Handbook.* Philadelphia, PA: FA Davis; 1983.
2. Gutierrez JE, Ordonez V. Normal sensory conduction in the infrapatellar branch of the saphenous nerve. Presented at the AAEM Annual Meeting; September 20, 1997.

SURAL NERVE

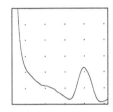

Typical waveform
appearance

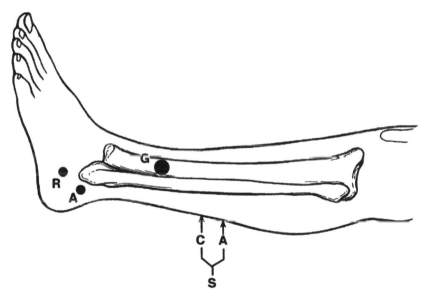

Electrode Placement

226

Position: This study is performed in the side-lying position.

Recording electrodes: A 3 cm bar electrode is used. Placement of the active electrode (A) is behind the lateral malleolus with the reference electrode (R) distal.

Ground electrode (G): Placement is between the stimulating and recording electrodes.

Stimulation point (S): The cathode (C) is placed 14 cm proximal to the active electrode in the midline or slightly lateral to the midline of the posterior lower leg. The anode (A) is proximal.

Machine settings: Sensitivity—2–5 µV/division, Low frequency filter—20 Hz, High frequency filter—2 kHz, Sweep speed—1 msec/division.

Nerve fibers tested: S1 and S2 nerve roots, through the anterior and posterior divisions of the lumbosacral plexus and the tibial and fibular nerves.

Reference values (1) (230 subjects) (skin temperature over the dorsum of the foot greater than or equal to 32°C):

Onset latency (msec)

Mean	SD	Range	Upper Reference Value
3.1	0.3	2.2–3.9	3.6

Peak latency (msec)

Mean	SD	Range	Upper Reference Value
3.8	0.3	2.8–4.6	4.5

Onset-to-peak amplitude (µV)

Mean	SD	Range	Lower Reference Value
17	10	2–56	4

Peak-to-peak amplitude (µV)

Mean	SD	Range	Lower Reference Value
21	12	3–69	4

Area under the curve from onset to positive peak (μVms)

Mean	SD	Range	Lower Reference Value
15	8	2–54	4

Duration (msec)

Mean	SD	Range	Upper Reference Value
1.6	0.3	1.0–2.1	2.1

Acceptable Differences

The upper limit of normal increase in onset latency from one side to the other is 0.4 msec.

The upper limit of normal increase in peak latency from one side to the other is 0.5 msec.

The upper limit of normal decrease in onset-to-peak amplitude from one side to the other is 72%.

The upper limit of normal decrease in peak-to-peak amplitude from one side to the other is 67%.

The upper limit of normal difference between sural and saphenous onset latency in the same limb is 0.3 msec in cases where the sural has the longer latency; it is 0.7 msec in cases where the saphenous latency is longer.

The upper limit of normal difference between sural and saphenous peak latency in the same limb is 0.5 msec in cases where the sural has the longer latency; it is 0.6 msec in cases where the saphenous latency is longer.

Sural/Radial Amplitude Ratio (2)

- Useful when the sural amplitude is "borderline normal."

- Sural/radial amplitude ratio (SRAR) <0.40 has a sensitivity of 90% and a specificity of 90% in detecting an axonal polyneuropathy. If SRAR of <0.21 is used then the specificity is 95%.

- SRAR is less dependent upon age than the sural nerve amplitude.

- Not to be used with superimposed sural or radial mononeuropathy.

Helpful Hints

- The stimulator may need to be moved slightly to one side or the other using the technique of "sliding" to obtain the optimum response.

- To minimize stimulus artifact the anode of the stimulator may need to be rotated while maintaining the cathode.

- The technique is best performed with the subject lying on his side; if performed when the patient is supine, the stimulation will often be too lateral.

- Occasionally, the responses may need to be electronically averaged to optimize the signal-to-noise ratio.

- Since the amplitude can be small it is important to use a 60 Hz notch filter.

- Prepping the skin with alcohol and abrasives is often helpful at eliciting small responses.

- Rotation of the stimulating electrode may be required to reduce the stimulation artifact.

Notes

REFERENCES

1. Buschbacher RM. Sural and saphenous 14-cm antidromic sensory nerve conduction studies. *Am J Phys Med Rehabil.* 2003;82(6):421–426.
2. Rutkove SB, Kothari MJ, Raynor EM, et al. Sural/radial amplitude ratio in the diagnosis of mild axonal polyneuropathy. *Muscle Nerve.* 1997;20(10):1236–1241.

ADDITIONAL READINGS

Barnett C, Perkins BA, Ngo M, et al. Sural-to-radial amplitude ratio in the diagnosis of diabetic sensorimotor polyneuropathy. *Muscle Nerve.* 2012;45(1):126–127.

Bye A, Fagan E. Nerve conduction studies of the sural nerve in childhood. *J Child Neurol.* 1988;3(2):94–99.

Esper GJ, Nardin RA, Benatar M, et al. Sural and radial nerve responses in healthy adults: diagnostic implications for polyneuropathy. *Muscle Nerve.* 2005;31(5):628–632.

Falco FJE, Hennessey WJ, Goldberg G, Braddom RL. Standardized nerve conduction studies in the lower limb of the healthy elderly. *Am J Phys Med Rehabil.* 1994;73:168–174.

Greathouse DG, Currier DP, Joseph BS, et al. Electrophysiological responses of human sural nerve to temperature. *Phys Ther.* 1989;69(11):914–922.

Hotritz SH, Krarup C. Conduction studies of the normal sural nerve. *Muscle Nerve.* 1992;15:374–383.

Killian JM, Foreman PJ. Clinical utility of dorsal sural nerve conduction studies. *Muscle Nerve.* 2001;24(6):817–820.

Kokotis P, Mandellos D, Papagianni A, Karandreas N. Normogram for determining lower limit of normal of the sural nerve. *Clin Neurophysiol.* 2010;121(4):561–563.

Plastaras CT, Marciniak CM, Sipple DP, et al. Effect of interelectrode distance on sural nerve action potential parameters. *Am J Phys Med Rehabil.* 2008;87(3):183–188.

Shin JB, Seong YJ, Lee HJ, et al. The usefulness of minimal F-wave latency and sural/radial amplitude ratio in diabetic polyneuropathy. *Yonsei Med J.* 2000;41(3):393–397.

Tavee JO, Polston D, Zhou L, et al. Sural sensory nerve action potential, epidermal nerve fiber density, and quantitative sudomotor axon reflex in the healthy elderly. *Muscle Nerve.* 2014;49(4):564–569.

Trojaborg WT, Moon A, Andersen BB, Trojaborg NS. Sural nerve conduction parameters in normal subjects related to age, gender, temperature and height: a reappraisal. *Muscle Nerve.* 1992;15(6):666–671.

Truong XT, Russo FI, Vagi I, Rippel DV. Conduction velocity in the proximal sural nerve. *Arch Phys Med Rehabil.* 1979;60:304–308.

Vrancken AF, Notermans NC, Wokke JH, Franssen H. The realistic yield of lower leg SNAP amplitudes and SRAR in the routine evaluation of chronic axonal polyneuropathies. *J Neurol*. 2008;255(8):1127–1135.

Wainapel SF, Kim DJ, Ebel A. Conduction studies of the saphenous nerve in healthy subjects. *Arch Phys Med Rehabil*. 1978;59:316–319.

SURAL SENSORY NERVE: LATERAL DORSAL CUTANEOUS BRANCH

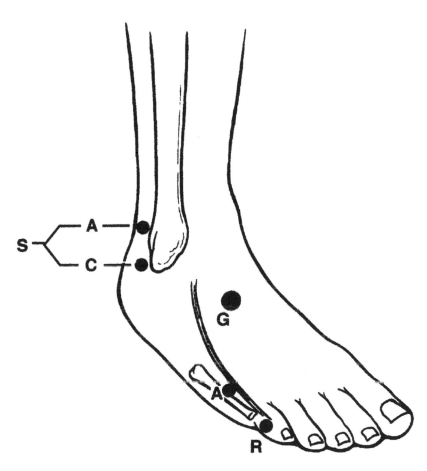

Electrode Placement

Position: This study is performed in the supine position.

Recording electrodes: Felt-tip electrodes with a fixed interelectrode distance of 37 mm were used in the cited study. Placement is such that the active electrode (A) is over the dorsolateral surface of the foot at the midpoint of the 5th metatarsal and just lateral to the extensor digitorum brevis tendon of the 5th toe. The reference electrode (R) is distal.

Ground electrode (G): Placement is on the dorsum of the foot.

Stimulation point (S): The cathode (C) is placed 12 cm proximal to the active electrode behind the lateral malleolus. The anode (A) is proximal.

Machine settings: Electronic averaging is used (5–10 stimuli). Sensitivity—5 μV/division, Low frequency filter—20 Hz, High frequency filter—2 kHz, Sweep speed—1 msec/division.

Nerve fibers tested: S1 and S2 nerve roots, through the anterior and posterior divisions of the lumbosacral plexus and the tibial and fibular nerves.

Reference values (1) (40 subjects) (skin temperature over the dorsum of the foot greater than or equal to 31°C):

Onset latency (msec)

Mean	SD	Range	Upper Reference Value
3.2	0.4	2.5–4.0	4.0

Peak latency (msec)

Mean	SD	Range	Upper Reference Value
3.9	0.5	3.0–4.9	4.9

Baseline-to-peak amplitude (μV)

Mean	SD	Range
5.8	2.1	3.0–11.0

Notes

REFERENCE

1. Lee HJ, Bach HJR, DeLisa JA. Lateral dorsal cutaneous branch of the sural nerve: standardization in nerve conduction study. *Am J Phys Med Rehabil.* 1992;71:318–320.

ADDITIONAL READING/ALTERNATE TECHNIQUE

Killian JM, Foreman PJ. Clinical utility of dorsal sural nerve conduction studies. *Muscle Nerve.* 2001;24:817–820.

TIBIAL MIXED NERVE (MEDIAL AND LATERAL PLANTAR BRANCHES)

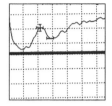

Typical waveform
appearance

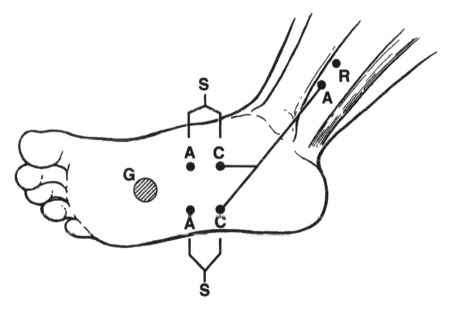

Electrode Placement

Position: This study is performed in the supine position. The examiner is usually at the foot of the bed.

Recording electrodes: A bar electrode is placed over the tibial nerve just proximal to the flexor retinaculum (proximal to a line from the posterior calcaneous to the medial malleolus. The active electrode (A) is distal and the reference electrode (R) is proximal (1).

Ground electrode (G): Placement is over the dorsum of the foot.

Stimulation points (S): The cathode (C) is placed 14 cm distal to the active recording electrode as shown in the accompanying figure for both the medial and lateral plantar branches. The anode (A) is distal. For the medial branch, the distance is measured 10 cm to the interspace between the 1st and 2nd metatarsals and then 4 cm distally. For the lateral branch, the stimulation site is between the 4th and 5th metatarsals (1).

Machine settings: Sensitivity—5–10 µV/division, Sweep speed—1 ms/division, Low frequency filter—32 Hz, High frequency filter—3.2 kHz.

Reference values (2) (41 subjects) (skin temperature over the tarsal tunnel and the medial and lateral sole of the foot ranges from 26°C–32°C):

Peak latency (msec)

	Mean	SD	Range	Upper Reference Value
Medial	3.16	0.26	2.6–3.7	3.7
Lateral	3.15	0.25	2.7–3.7	3.7

Amplitude (µV)

	Range
Medial	10–30
Lateral	8–20

Helpful Hints

- Although technically a mixed nerve study, this technique approximates a sensory study.

- Firm pressure should be exerted on the stimulating and recording electrodes.

- Stimulus artifact may interfere with the recording, especially in persons with thick plantar skin. Prepping the skin can be helpful.

- This response is often difficult to elicit even in normal subjects. Unelicitable waveforms must be interpreted with caution.

- Tarsal tunnel syndrome (TTS) can be difficult to diagnose: clinical and electrophysiologic corroboration is important. Conventional electrodiagnostic techniques are insensitive: motor latency abnormalities exist in only 52%; sensory responses are frequently absent (a nonlocalizing finding) (3).

Notes

REFERENCES

1. Dumitru D. Nerve conduction studies. In: Dumitru D, *Electrodiagnostic Medicine*, 2nd ed. Philadelphia, PA: Hanley and Belfus; 2002.
2. Saeed MA, Gatens PF. Compound nerve action potentials of the medial and lateral plantar nerves through the tarsal tunnel. *Arch Phys Med Rehabil.* 1982;63:304–307.
3. David WS, Doyle JJ. Segmental near nerve sensory conduction studies of the medial and lateral plantar nerve. *Electromyogr Clin Neurophysiol.* 1996;36:411–417.

ADDITIONAL READINGS/ALTERNATE TECHNIQUES

Cape CA. Sensory nerve action potentials of the peroneal, sural and tibial nerves. *Am J Phys Med.* 1971;50:220–229.

Oh SJ, Sarala PK, Kuba T, Elmore RS. Tarsal tunnel syndrome: electrophysiological study. *Ann Neurol.* 1979;5:327–330.

CHAPTER 5

HEAD AND NECK STUDIES

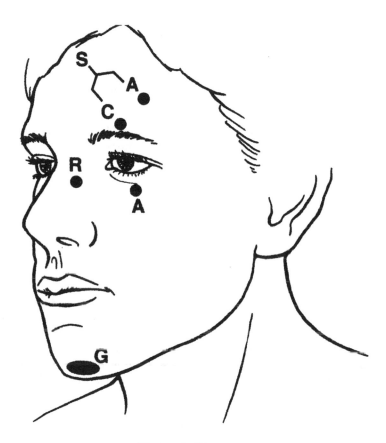

Electrode Placement

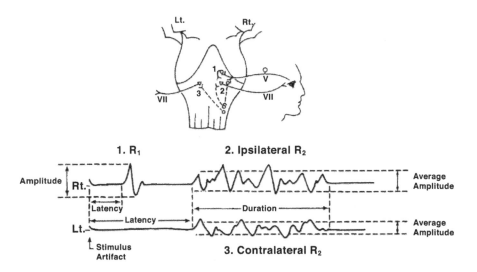

1. R_1 2. Ipsilateral R_2 3. Contralateral R_2

From *Electrodiagnosis in Diseases of Nerve and Muscle*, 3rd ed., by Jun Kimura, copyright © 2001 by Oxford University Press, Inc. Used by permission of Oxford University Press, Inc.

Active electrode (A): Placement is over the lower lateral orbicularis oculi muscle bilaterally (1).

Reference electrode (R): Placement is over the temple or the lateral surface of the nose above the nasalis muscle (1,2).

Ground electrode (G): Placement is under the chin or on the forehead or cheek (1,2).

Stimulation point (S): Stimulation is applied with the cathode (C) over the supraorbital nerve at the supraorbital notch (which can be palpated). The anode (A) is superiolateral. (Direct stimulation can also be applied to the facial nerve as it exits the stylomastoid foramen—see section on cranial nerve [CN] VII) (1,2).

Machine settings: Sensitivity—50 to 200 μV/division, Low frequency filter—20 Hz, High frequency filter—10 kHz, Sweep speed—10 msc/division (1,2).

Nerve fibers tested: Afferent CN V and efferent CN VII fibers, as well as their central connections.

Reference values (1) (83 subjects) (Upper limit of normal = mean + 3 SD, temperature not reported):

Direct latency (D) to facial nerve stimulation (ms)

Mean	SD	Upper Reference Value
2.9	0.4	4.1

R1 onset latency (ms)

Mean	SD	Upper Reference Value
10.5	0.8	13.0

Ipsilateral R2 latency (ms)

Mean	SD	Upper Reference Value
30.5	3.4	40

Contralateral R2 latency (ms)

Mean	SD	Upper Reference Value
30.5	4.4	41

Acceptable Differences

The upper limit of normal side-to-side difference in direct response latency (D) is 0.6 ms.

The upper limit of normal side to side difference in R1 latency is 1.2 ms (±3 SD).

The upper limit of normal side-to-side difference in R2 latency evoked by stimulation on one side (dual channel recording) is 5 ms. If the R2 is recorded by first stimulating one side and then the other (single channel recording), the upper limit of normal difference is 7 ms.

Helpful Hints

- The subject should be relaxed.

- The R2 latency may be variable.

- Several blink responses should be tested and the shortest latencies chosen. Kimura recommends that at least eight trials be performed (1).

- Latency should be measured to the first deflection from the baseline.

- Excessive numbers of stimuli may lead to habituation and should be avoided.

- A ratio of R1 latency (R) to the direct response latency (D) to facial nerve stimulation (see section on CN VII) can be calculated. This R/D ratio should not fall outside the range of 2.6 to 4.6 (1). A larger ratio, with a normal D, is indicative of slowing of the trigeminal portion of the arc. If the R/D ratio is low, it is indicative of slowing of the facial nerve component.

- Care should be taken to aim the anode away from the contralateral side so that bilateral stimulation is not performed inadvertently.

- In 5% to 10% of normal subjects paired stimuli are necessary to record a stable R1 (1).

- A glabellar tap with a special hammer can be used instead of electrical stimulation.

- In diabetic patients the blink reflex can be utilized to assist in the early diagnosis of cranial neuropathy. Both R1 and R2 latencies will be prolonged. This can reflect involvement of both CN V and VII (3). The blink reflex is also of value in detection of clinically silent intraaxial brainstem functional abnormalities or extraaxial lesions in diabetic patients before the development of peripheral neuropathy.

- In hemifacial spasm, the pathophysiological mechanisms underlying the generation of abnormal responses include lateral spread of ephaptic activity between neighboring fibers of the facial nerve and hyperexcitability of facial motorneurons. The blink reflex can be used to quantify the extent of this abnormality. In addition, when the R1 has a very short latency (approximately 10–14 ms), this likely represents the component of the orbicularis oris response that was likely generated by antidromic conduction in facial nerve motor axons and/or by axono-axonal activation of the fibers innervating the lower facial muscles. It also probably represents that the motor axono-axonal responses are generated by stimulation of facial nerve terminals (4).

Notes _____

_____

_____

_____

_____

_____

_____

_____

_____

_____

_____

_____

_____

_____

_____

_____

_____

REFERENCES

1. Kimura J. *Electrodiagnosis in Diseases of Nerve and Muscle: Principles and Practice.* 3rd ed. New York, NY: Oxford University Press; 2013.
2. Dumitru D. *Electrodiagnostic Medicine.* 2nd ed. Philadelphia, PA: Hanley & Belfus; 2002.
3. Guney F, Demir O, Gonen MS. Blink reflex alterations in diabetic patients with and without polyneuropathy. *Int J Neurosci.* 2008;118(9):1287–1298.
4. Montero J, Junyent J, Calopa M, et al. Electrophysiological study of ephaptic axono-axonal responses in hemifacial spasm. *Muscle Nerve.* 2007;35(2):184–188.

ADDITIONAL READINGS/ALTERNATE TECHNIQUES

Dumitru D, Walsh NE, Porter LD. Electrophysiological evaluation of the facial nerve in Bell's palsy. A review. *Am J Phys Med Rehabil.* 1988;67:137–144.

Ellrich J, Hopf HC. The R3 component of the blink reflex: normative data and application in spinal lesions. *Electroencephalogr Clin Neurophysiol.* 1996;101:349–354.

Kazem SS, Behzad D. Role of blink reflex in diagnosis of subclinical cranial neuropathy in diabetes type II. *Am J Phys Med Rehabil.* 2006;85(5):449–452.

Kimura J, Powers JM, Van Allen MW. Reflex response of orbicularis oculi muscle to supraorbital nerve stimulation. *Arch Neurol.* 1969;21:193–199.

Kimura J, Bodensteiner J, Yamada T. Electrically elicited blink reflex in normal neonates. *Arch Neurol.* 1977;34:246–249.

Ma DM, Liveson JA. *Nerve Conduction Handbook.* Philadelphia, PA: FA Davis; 1983.

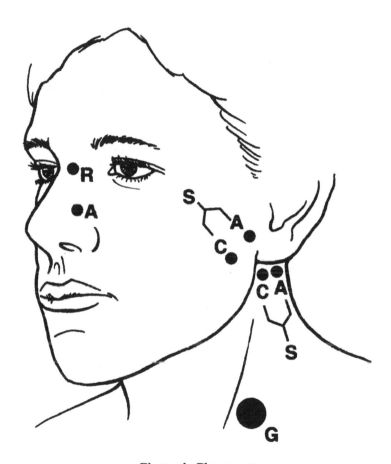

Electrode Placement

Position: This study is performed in the seated position.

Active electrode (A): Placement can be over the nasalis, orbicularis oris, orbicularis oculi, or levator labii superioris (or essentially any muscle innervated by the nerve). For recording from the nasalis, the active electrode is placed on the lateral mid-nose. The subject may "wrinkle the nose" and the electrode is placed on the most prominent bulge of the muscle. For the orbicularis oculi the active electrode is placed under the eye in line with the pupil. An alternate position is at the lateral border of the eye. For the orbicularis oris the active electrode is placed lateral to the angle of the mouth (1–4).

Reference electrode (R): Placement is on the tip or bridge of the nose (1,2). For nasalis recording it may also be placed on the contralateral nasalis muscle.

Ground electrode (G): Placement is over the base of the neck or on the cheek (1,2).

Stimulation point (S): Preauricular stimulation is performed with the cathode (C) just anterior to the lower ear over the substance of the parotid gland and several centimeters superior to the angle of the mandible. Postauricular stimulation is performed at the stylomastoid foramen by placing the cathode just behind the lower ear, below the mastoid process and behind the neck of the mandible. The anode (A) is posterior (1,2).

Machine settings: Sensitivity—200 to 1,000 µV/division, Low frequency filter—8 Hz, High frequency filter—8 kHz, Sweep speed—1 to 2 ms/division (2).

Nerve fibers tested: CN VII efferent motor fibers.

Reference values (1) (44 subjects) (room temperature 23°C–26°C):

Preauricular stimulation latency to the nasalis (ms)

Mean	SD	Range
3.57	0.35	2.8–4.1

Postauricular stimulation latency to the nasalis (ms)

Mean	SD	Range
3.88	0.36	3.2–4.4

Acceptable Difference

A side-to-side difference in amplitude of greater than 50% is suggestive of pathology, but the waveform must be similar on both sides (2).

Helpful Hints

- Serial study of the amplitude may be clinically useful.

- Recordings may be made from any CN VII muscle. Surface recording is preferred as this allows assessment of amplitude. The amplitude should be measured from onset to the peak of the negative wave. The needle recording technique has also been described (3,4). With concentric needle recording from the orbicularis oris and stimulation with the cathode over the stylomastoid foramen, the latency in 40 adult subjects was reported as 4.0 ± 0.5 ms (3).

- The motor points in the facial muscles may be poorly defined and an initially negative deflection may not be obtained. If this is the case, latency should be recorded at the initial deflection from baseline (2).

- In cases of CN VII pathology, direct activation of the masseter, especially when recording from orbicularis oris or when using high levels of stimulation, can give a false volume conducted response. This muscle can be palpated to ensure that this is not occurring. If this is a confounding factor, the facial nerve can be stimulated under the zygoma. This results in a shorter latency recording, but side to side comparisons can still be made (2).

Notes

REFERENCES

1. Ma DM, Liveson JA. *Nerve Conduction Handbook.* Philadelphia, PA: FA Davis; 1983.
2. Dumitru D. *Electrodiagnostic Medicine.* 2nd ed. Philadelphia, PA: Hanley & Belfus; 2002.
3. Taylor N, Jebsen RH, Tenckhoff HA. Facial nerve conduction latency in chronic renal insufficiency. *Arch Phys Med Rehabil.* 1970;51:259–263.
4. Waylonis GW, Johnson EW. Facial nerve conduction delay. *Arch Phys Med Rehabil.* 1964;45:539–547.

ADDITIONAL READINGS/ALTERNATE TECHNIQUES

Bhargava A, Banakar BF, Pujar GS, Khichar S. A study of guillain barre syndrome with reference to cranial neuropathy and its prognostic implications. *J Neurosci Rural Pract.* 2014;5(Suppl 1):S43–S47.

Boongird P, Vejjajiva A. Electrophysiological findings and prognosis in Bell's palsy. *Muscle Nerve.* 1978;1(6):461–466.

DeMeirsman J, Claes G, Geerdens L. Normal latency value of the facial nerve with detection in the posterior auricular muscle and normal amplitude value of the evoked action potential. *Electromyogr Clin Neurophysiol.* 1980;20:481–485.

Dumitru D, Walsh NE, Porter LD. Electrophysiological evaluation of the facial nerve in Bell's palsy. *Am J Phys Med Rehabil.* 1988;67:137–144.

Kiziltan ME, Uluduz D, Yaman M, Uzun N. Electrophysiological findings of acute peripheral facial palsy in diabetic and non-diabetic patients. *Neurosci Lett.* 2007;418(3):222–226.

Typical waveform
appearance

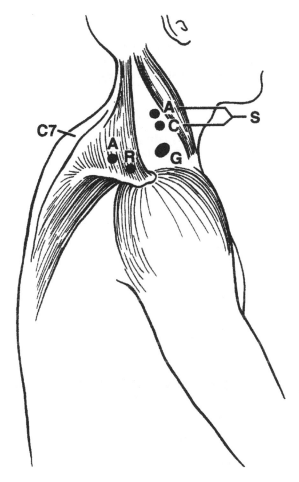

Electrode Placement

Position: This study is performed in the seated position.

Active electrode (A): Placement is over the upper trapezius, about 9 cm lateral to the 7th cervical spinous process.

Reference electrode (R): Placement is 3 cm lateral to the active electrode.

Ground electrode (G): Placement is between the stimulating and recording electrodes.

Stimulation point (S): The cathode (C) is placed in the posterior triangle of the neck, 1 to 2 cm posterior to the posterior border sternocleidomastoid muscle and slightly above the midpoint of this muscle. This is a point halfway between the mastoid process and the suprasternal notch. The anode (A) is superior (1,2).

Nerve fibers tested: CN XI.

Machine settings: Sensitivity—1 mV/division, with a Sweep speed of 1 to 2 ms/division (2), Low frequency filter—2–3 Hz, High frequency filter—10 kHz.

Reference values (1) (28 subjects) (room temperature 23°C–26°C):

Onset latency (ms)

Mean	SD	Range
2.3	0.4	1.7–3.0

Peak-to-peak amplitude (mV)

>3–4

Helpful Hints

- Care should be taken not to stimulate the brachial plexus. Muscle contraction in the arm is a clinical clue to overstimulation.
- The shoulder should shrug with activation of CN XI.

Notes

REFERENCES

1. Ma DM, Liveson JA. *Nerve Conduction Handbook*. Philadelphia, PA: FA Davis; 1983.
2. Dumitru D. *Electrodiagnostic Medicine*. 2nd ed. Philadelphia, PA: Hanley & Belfus; 2002.

ADDITIONAL READINGS/ALTERNATE TECHNIQUES

Green RF, Brien M. Accessory nerve latency to the middle and lower trapezius. *Arch Phys Med Rehabil*. 1985;66:23–24.

LoMonaco M, DiPasqua PG, Tonali P. Conduction studies along the accessory, long thoracic, dorsal scapular, and thoracodorsal nerves. *Acta Neurol Scand*. 1983;68:171–176.

Petrera JE, Trojaborg W. Conduction studies along the accessory nreve and follow-up of patients with trapezius palsy. *J Neurol Neurosurg Psychiatry*. 1984;47(6):630–636.

Shankar K, Means KM. Accessory nerve conduction in neck dissection subjects. *Arch Phys Med Rehabil*. 1990;71:403–405.

GREATER AURICULAR SENSORY NERVE

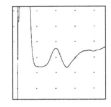

Typical waveform
appearance

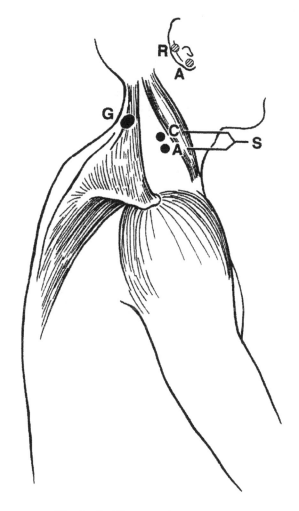

Electrode Placement

Position: This study is performed in the seated position.

Recording electrodes: Placement is on the back of the earlobe, 2 cm apart. The active electrode (A) is inferior.

Ground electrode (G): Placement is on the back of the neck.

Stimulation point (S): Stimulation is applied along the posterior border of the sternocleidomastoid muscle, with the cathode (C) superior and located 8 cm from the active electrode. The anode (A) is inferior.

Machine settings: Low frequency filter—32 Hz, High frequency filter—3.2 kHz, Sweep speed—1 ms/division, Sensitivity—20 µV/division.

Nerve fibers tested: C2 and C3 nerve roots.

Reference values (1) (64 nerves in 32 subjects, ranging in age from 14 to 88 years) (skin temperature maintained at or above 33°C):

Onset latency (ms)

Mean	SD	Upper Reference Value
1.34	0.15	1.6

Peak latency (ms)

Mean	SD	Upper Reference Value
1.89	0.21	2.3

Peak-to-peak amplitude (µV)

Mean	SD
22.4	8.93

Duration (ms) (2)

Mean	SD	Upper Reference Value
0.8	0.2	1.2

Helpful Hints

- This study may be difficult to perform in those subjects who are heavy-set with short necks.

- Recording may be done from the mastoid process (2).

- Palliyath found similar peak latencies of 1.7 ± 0.2 ms; onset to peak amplitudes were 12.7 ± 4.1 μV (2).

REFERENCES

1. Kimura I, Seki H, Sasso S, Ayyar DR. The great auricular nerve conduction study: a technique normative data and clinical usefulness. *Electromyogr Clin Neurophysiol.* 1987;27:39–43.

2. Palliyath SK. A technique for studying the greater auricular nerve conduction velocity. *Muscle Nerve.* 1984;7:232–234.

CHAPTER 6

ROOT STIMULATION AND PUDENDAL NERVE STUDIES

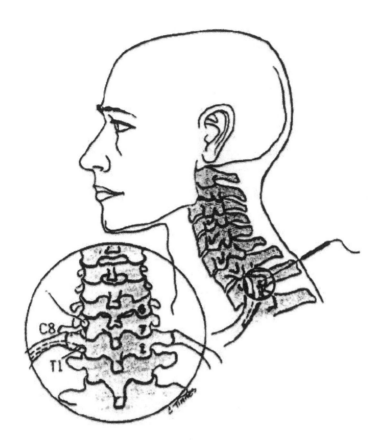

Needle placement for stimulating the C-8 and T-1 spinal nerves for evaluation of the lower trunk and medial cord of the brachial plexus. (*From* McLean IC: nerve root stimulation to evaluate conduction across the brachial and lumbosacral plexuses. *In* Third Annual Continuing Education Course [Sept. 25, 1980]: Recent Advances in Clinical Electromyography. Philadelphia, AANEM, 1980, pp 51-55. Copyright © 1980 American Association of Electromyography and Electrodiagnosis, with permission.)

Recording electrodes: Depending on which nerve roots are being tested, placement is over the motor points of the abductor digiti minimi (C8–T1 roots), biceps (C5–C6 roots), or triceps (C6–C8 roots) muscles. The reference electrode is placed over a distal tendon (1).

Stimulation point (S): Stimulation is performed with a 50 mm monopolar needle electrode. This cathode is inserted perpendicular to the skin approximately 1 cm lateral to the spinous processes so that the tip rests on the vertebral laminae. For the C5/C6 root, the needle is placed at the level of the C5 vertebra. For the C6/C7/C8 roots, the needle is placed at the level of the C6 vertebra. The C8/T1 roots are stimulated at the level of the C7 vertebra. The anode is a surface electrode and is placed 1 cm caudal and slightly medial to the cathode.

Machine settings: Low frequency filter—8 Hz, High frequency filter—8 kHz, Sensitivity—5 mV/division, Sweep speed—2 sec/division for proximal muscles and 5 sec/division for distal muscles.

Acceptable Differences: (1) (30 Root Pairs in 12 Subjects)

The upper limit of normal latency asymmetry from side-to-side is 1.0 ms.

The upper limit of normal amplitude asymmetry (percentage reduction from the larger to the smaller value) from side-to-side is 20%.

Vucic et al. (2) studied 21 normal subjects and found mean compound motor action potential onset-latencies were: APB 14 +/– 1.5 ms; ADM 14.2 +/– 1.5 ms; biceps 5.4 +/– 0.6 ms; triceps 5.4 +/– 1.0 ms. Onset-latency significantly correlated with height for all nerves. In addition, the mean numeric rating scale (NRS) score was 3.8 +/– 1.2 suggesting that the procedure was well tolerated.

Cervical root stimulation can also be used for primary demyelinating neuropathies (PDP) and motor neuron disease (MND): Vucic et al. (3) found mean onset-latency was significantly prolonged in PDP patients. The optimal onset-latency cutoff necessary to distinguish PDP from MND and controls was 17.5 ms for the abductor pollicis brevis and abductor digiti minimi, and 7 ms for biceps and triceps. Mean reduction in proximal to distal CMAP amplitude to APB and ADM was significantly greater in PDP patients, with an optimal cutoff in proximal to distal CMAP amplitude reduction necessary to distinguish PDP from MND and healthy controls being 45%.

Helpful Hints

- Needle recording has also been recommended when recording from the triceps (2). Reliable amplitude measurements can, however, only be made using surface electrode recording.

- A slightly different stimulation procedure has also been studied. Stimulation is similar to that previously described, but the monopolar needle electrode is inserted 1 to 2 cm lateral and inferior to the corresponding spinous processes. The needle is inserted until bone is encountered and is then withdrawn several millimeters. A stimulus duration of 0.05 ms is usually adequate. The anode can be either a surface electrode or another monopolar needle electrode inserted at the same site contralaterally (4–6).

- This is a nonspecific test and does not alone make the diagnosis of radiculopathy. Stimulation likely occurs at the neural foramen, distal to typical sites of compression. Any other pathology along the course of the nerve can cause slowing, so other pathology needs to be ruled out.

- Side-to-side comparison is limited if pathology is bilateral.

- A reduction in amplitude of 50% or more between limb stimulation and root stimulation has been used to define a proximal conduction block. The limb stimulation is applied above the common sites of nerve compression (for example, for the ulnar nerve it is applied above the elbow) (7).

Notes

REFERENCES

1. Berger AR, Busis NA, Logigian EL, et al. Cervical root stimulation in the diagnosis of radiculopathy. *Neurology.* 1987;37:329–332.
2. Vucic S, Cairns KD, Black KR, et al. Cervical nerve root stimulation. Part 1: technical aspects and normal data. *Clin Neurophysiol.* 2006;117(2):392–397.
3. Vucic S, Black K, Siao Tick Chong P, Cros D. Cervical nerve root stimulation. Part II: findings in primary demyelinating neuropathies and motor neuron disease. *Clin Neurophysiol.* 2006;117(2):398–404.
4. Dumitru D. *Electrodiagnostic medicine.* 2nd ed. Philadelphia, PA: Hanley & Belfus; 2002.
5. Kraft GH, Johnson EW. American Association of Electrodiagnostic Medicine. Proximal motor nerve conduction and late responses: an AAEM workshop. Rochester, MN: American Association of Electrodiagnostic Medicine; 1986:1–12.
6. MacLean IC. Spinal nerve stimulation. In: AAEM Course B: nerve conduction studies—a review. Rochester, MN: American Association of Electrodiagnostic Medicine; 1988.
7. Menkes DL, Hood DC, Ballesteros RA, Williams DA. Root stimulation improves the detection of acquired demyelinating polyneuropathies. *Muscle Nerve.* 1988;21:298–308.

ADDITIONAL READINGS/ALTERNATE TECHNIQUES

Evans BA, Daube JR, Litchy WJ. A comparison of magnetic and electrical stimulation of spinal nerves. *Muscle Nerve.* 1990;13:414–420.

Livingstone EF, DeLisa JA, Halar EM. Electrodiagnostic values through the thoracic outlet using C8 root needle studies, F-waves, and cervical somatosensory evoked potentials. *Arch Phys Med Rehabil.* 1984;65:726–730.

Tsai CP, Huang CI, Wang V, et al. Evaluation of cervical radiculopathy by cervical root stimulation. *Electromyogr Clin Neurophysiol.* 1994;34:363–366.

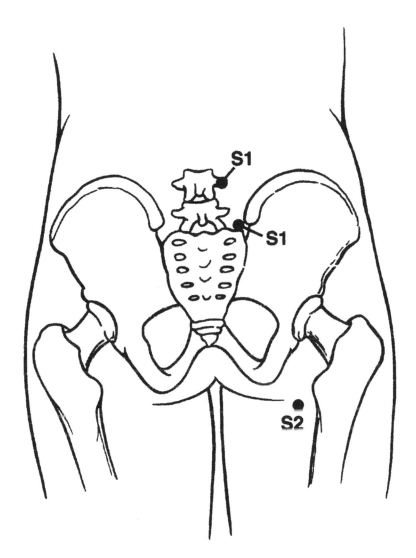

Electrode Placement

Recording electrodes: The active and reference electrodes can be placed on any appropriate muscle of the lower extremity (1–3). The active electrode is placed over the motor point or central portion of the muscle. The reference electrode is placed over the distal tendinous insertion of that muscle. Needle recording may be used.

Ground electrode: Placement is between the stimulating and recording electrodes.

Stimulation point 1 (S1): A 50 to 75 mm monopolar needle electrode is used as the cathode. To access the L2/L3/L4 nerve roots, the needle is inserted 2 to 2.5 cm lateral to the spinous process of the L4 vertebral body. The needle is positioned on the periosteum of the vertebral arch overlying the L4 root. The anode is also a needle electrode and is located on the contralateral side in a similar position (1,2).

To access the L5/S1 nerve roots, a similar setup is used but the needle electrodes are inserted just medial and a bit caudal to the posterior superior iliac spine (1,2).

An alternate technique for the L5/S1 root has been described, which involves placing a superficial electrode on the abdomen as the anode. It is placed opposite the cathode (3). The placement of the stimulating electrodes can be confirmed by ultrasound.

Stimulation point 2 (S2) (optional): For the L2/L3/L4 nerve roots, a second stimulus can be applied to the femoral nerve at the inguinal region (see section on femoral nerve). For the L5/S1 roots, a second stimulus can be applied to the sciatic nerve at the gluteal fold (see section on sciatic nerve). The latency from S2 stimulation is subtracted from the S1 latency to calculate a trans-plexus conduction time (1,2). The placement of these can be confirmed by ultrasound.

Machine settings: Sensitivity—2 to 5 mV/division, Low frequency filter—10 Hz, High frequency filter—10 kHz, Sweep speed—2 to 5 msec/division (1).

Reference values:

L5/S1 latency to the soleus (msec) (3)

Mean	SD
15.4	1.3

Side-to-side difference: 0.2 msec (range 0.0–0.8)

Latency to tibialis anterior (msec) (4) (12 subjects)

Mean	SD	Range
13.5	1.2	11.4–15.9

Latency to tibialis anterior (msec) (5) (30 subjects)

Mean	SD	Range
12.4	1.3	10.8–13.7

Side-to-side difference: mean 0.3 ± 0.2 msec (range 0.0–0.9)
      Upper limit of normal difference: <0.7 msec

Latency to flexor hallucis brevis (msec) (4) (14 subjects)

Mean	SD	Range
25.1	2.0	21.7–29.7

L2/L3/L4 Trans-plexus conduction time recording from the vastus medialis (msec) (1,2)

Mean	SD	Range
3.4	0.6	2.0–4.4

Side-to-side difference: 0.0 to 0.9 msec

L5/S1 Trans-plexus conduction time recording from the abductor hallucis (msec) (1,2)

Mean	SD	Range
3.9	0.7	2.5–4.9

Side-to-side difference: 0.0 to 1.0 msec

Amplitude to tibialis anterior (mV) (5) (30 subjects)

Mean	SD	Range
5.7	2.4	3.2–10.5

Side-to-side difference: mean 3.8% ± 2.9 (range 1.4–12.7)
      Upper limit of normal difference: 9.6%

Area to tibialis anterior (mVms) (5) (30 subjects)

Mean	SD	Range
25.2	9.6	15.7–41.3

Side-to-side difference: 6.1% ± 3.1 (range 3.6–17.1)
    Upper limit of normal difference: 12.3%

Helpful Hint

- A reduction in amplitude of 50% or more between limb stimulation and root stimulation has been used to define a proximal conduction block. The limb stimulation is applied above the common sites of nerve compression (for example, for the fibular nerve it is applied above the knee) (6).

Notes

_____

_____

_____

_____

_____

REFERENCES

1. Dumitru D. *Electrodiagnostic medicine*. 2nd ed. Philadelphia, PA: Hanley & Belfus; 2002.
2. MacLean IC. Spinal nerve stimulation. In: AAEM Course B: nerve conduction studies—a review. Rochester, MN: American Association of Electrodiagnostic Medicine; 1988.
3. Kraft GH, Johnson EW. American Association of Electrodiagnostic Medicine. Proximal motor nerve conduction and late responses: an AAEM workshop. Rochester, MN: American Association of Electrodiagnostic Medicine; 1986:1–12.
4. Macdonnell RAL, Cros D, Shahani BT. Lumbosacral nerve root stimulation comparing electrical with surface magnetic coil techniques. *Muscle Nerve*. 1992;15:885–890.

5. Chang CW, Lien IN. Spinal nerve stimulation in the diagnosis of lumbosacral radiculopathy. *Am J Phys Med Rehabil.* 1990;69:318–322.

6. Menkes DL, Hood DC, Ballesteros RA, Williams DA. Root stimulation improves the detection of acquired demyelinating polyneuropathies. *Muscle Nerve.* 1988;21:298–308.

ADDITIONAL READINGS/ALTERNATE TECHNIQUE

Cao X, Zhao X, Xu J, et al. Ultrasound guided technology versus stimulation for sciatic nerve block: a meta-analysis. *Int J Clin Exp Med.* 2015;8(1):273–280.

Ghugare BW, Singh RK, Patond KR, Joshi MU. Assessment of nerve conduction study to establish most common electrophysiological predictor of lumbosacral radiculopathy amoung radiologically diagnosed L5S1 neural foramena compression cases. *Indian J Physiol Pharmacol.* 2013;57(2):209–213.

Sato M, Mikawa Y, Matuda A. Ultrasound and electrical nerve stimulation-guided S1 nerve root block. *J Anesth.* 2013;27(5):775–777.

Troni W, Bianco C, Moja MC, Dotta M. Improved methodology for lumbosacral nerve root stimulation. *Muscle Nerve.* 1996;19:595–604.

PUDENDAL NERVE STUDIES

Position: This nerve is examined in the supine position with hips and knees flexed and legs abducted.

Recording electrodes: One cm diameter electrodes are placed over the radial creases of the external anal sphincter at the 9 o'clock position (for the right sided response) or the 3 o'clock position (for the left sided response). The reference electrode is placed in the midline several centimeters away from the external anal sphincter on the gluteal fold.

Stimulation point (S): Stimulation occurs on each side via a St. Mark's disposable electrode, with the cathode and anode at the end of a gloved finger placed at the ischial spine via a transvaginal approach.

Machine settings: Low frequency filter—10 Hz, High frequency filter—10 kHz. Sensitivity 50 µV/division; Sweep speed 2 msec/division. Stimulus duration — 0.05 msec, Stimulus intensity 10–15 mA. Multiple responses are averaged to obtain stable values.

Reference values (1) (42 subjects):

Onset latency (msec)

	Mean	*Range*	*Upper Limit of Normal*
All Subjects	1.94	1.55–2.54	2.23
< 40 y/o	1.91	1.64–2.35	2.16
40–59 y/o	1.93	1.55–2.54	2.26
≥ 60 y/o	2.10	1.90–2.30	2.33

Baseline-to-peak amplitude (µV)

	Mean	Range	Lower Limit of Normal
All Subjects	101	20–260	48
< 40 y/o	119	25–260	56
40–59 y/o	87	20–210	44
≥ 60 y/o	80	60–115	55

Notes

REFERENCE

1. Olsen AL, Ross M, Stansfield RB, Kreiter C. Pelvic floor nerve conduction studies: Establishing clinically relevant normative data. *Am J Obstet Gynecol.* 2003;189:1114–1119.

ADDITIONAL READINGS

Benson J. Clinical neurophysiological techniques in urinary, and fecal incontinence. *In: Ostergard DR, Bent AE, editors. Urogynecology and urodynamics: theory and practice. 4th ed. Baltimore (MD): Williams & Wilkins;* 1996. p. 240. p. 225–250.

Dick HC, Bradley WE, Scott FB, Timm GW. Pudendal sexual reflexes: electrophysiologic investigations. *Urology.* 1974;3:376–379.

Kiff ES, Swash M. Slowed conduction in the pudendal nerves in idiopathic (neurogenic) faecal incontinence. *Br J Surg.* 1984;71:614–616.

Snooks SJ, Swash M. Perineal nerve and transcutaneous spinal stimulation: new methods for investigation of the urethral striated sphincter musculature. *Br J Urol.* 1984;56:406–409.

Tetzschner T, Sorensen M, Lose G, Christiansen J. Vaginal pudendal nerve stimulation: a new technique for assessment of pudendal nerve terminal motor latency. *Acta Obstet Gynecol Scand.* 1997;76:294–299.

CHAPTER 7

OTHER STUDIES OF INTEREST

The following is a list of some other nerve conduction tests that have been published. This list obviously is not all-inclusive, but it does give the reader references for other studies that may be necessary from time to time. It is anticipated that most of these studies will not be performed routinely by most electrodiagnosticians. As a rule, these studies also require more in-depth reading, study, and practice than is possible to summarize in the format of the preceding sections.

Autonomic Nervous System

1. Ravits JM. AAEM minimonograph #48: autonomic nervous system testing. *Muscle Nerve.* 1997;20(8):919–937.
2. Hilz MJ, Dutsch M. Quantitative studies of autonomic function. *Muscle Nerve.* 2006;33(1):6–20.
3. Floeter MK. Cutaneous silent periods. *Muscle Nerve.* 2003;28(4):391–401.

Axillary F-Loop/Central Latency

1. Hong CZ, Joynt RL, Lin JC, et al. Axillary F-loop latency of ulnar nerve in normal young adults. *Arch Phys Med Rehabil.* 1981;62:565–569.
2. Hong CZ, Batkin F, Yu J, San Luis EB. Averaged axillary F-loop latency of median and ulnar nerves. *Arch Phys Med Rehabil.* 1988;69(9):685–688.
3. Wu Y, Kunz JRM, Putnam TD, Stratigos JS. Axillary F central latency: simple electrodiagnostic technique for proximal neuropathy. *Arch Phys Med Rehabil.* 1983;64:117–120.

Axillary Sensory Nerve Conduction

1. Karandreas N, Papatheodorou A, Triantaphilos I, et al. Sensory nerve conduction studies of the less frequently examined nerves. *Electromyogr Clin Neurophysiol.* 1995;35:169–173.

Bulbocavernosus Reflex/Perineal/Pudendal Nerve Conduction

1. Dick HC, Bradley WE, Scott FB, Timm GW. Pudendal sexual reflexes: electrophysiologic investigations. *Urology.* 1974;3:376–379.
2. Siroky MB, Sax DS, Krane RJ. Sacral signal tracing: the electrophysiology of the bulbocavernosus reflex. *J Urol.* 1979;122:661–664.
3. Kiff ES, Swash M. Slowed conduction in the pudendal nerves in idiopathic (neurogenic) faecal incontinence. *Br J Surg.* 1984;71:614–616.

4. Snooks SJ, Swash M. Perineal nerve and transcutaneous spinal stimulation: new methods for investigation of the urethral striated sphincter musculature. *Br J Urol.* 1984;56:406–409.

5. Tetzschner T, Sorensen M, Lose G, Christiansen J. Vaginal pudendal nerve stimulation: a new technique for assessment of pudendal nerve terminal motor latency. *Acta Obstet Gynecol Scand.* 1997;76:294–299.

6. Voyvodic F, Schloithe AC, Wattchow DA, et al. Delayed pudendal nerve conduction and endosonographic appearance of the anal sphincter complex. *Dis Colon Rectum.* 2000;43(12):1689–1694.

7. Fishel B, Chen J, Alon M, et al. Pudendal nerve conduction to evaluate organic erectile dysfunction. *Am J Phys Med Rehabil.* 2001;80(12):885–888.

Dorsal Nerve of the Penis

1. Bradley WE, Lin JTY, Johnson B. Measurement of the conduction velocity of the dorsal nerve of the penis. *J Urol.* 1984;131:1127–1129.

2. Clawson DR, Cardenas DD. Dorsal nerve of the penis nerve conduction velocity: a new technique. *Muscle Nerve.* 1991;14:845–849.

3. Fanciullacci F, Colpi GM, Beretta G, et al. Nerve conduction velocity of the dorsal nerve of the penis: a modified technique. *Urology.* 1991;38(6):540–547.

4. Herbaut AG, Sattar AA, Salpigides G, et al. Sensory conduction velocity of dorsal nerve of the penis during pharmacoerection: a more physiological technique? *Eur Urol.* 1996;30:60–64.

Dorsal Rami, Sensory Conduction

1. Singh AP, Sommer HM. Sensory nerve conduction studies of the L-1/L-2 dorsal rami. *Arch Phys Med Rehabil.* 1996;77:913–915.

Dorsal Scapular Nerve Motor Conduction

1. LoMonaco M, DiPasqua RG, Tonali P. Conduction studies along the accessory, long thoracic, dorsal scapular, and thoracodorsal nerves. *Acta Neurol Scand.* 1983;68:171–176.

Femoral/Obturator Nerves

1. Uludag B, Ertekin C, Turman B, et al. Proximal and distal motor nerve conduction in obturator and femoral nerves. *Arch Phys Med Rehabil.* 2000;81:1166–1170.

Hypoglossal Motor Nerve Conduction

1. Redmond MD, DiBenedetto M. Electrodiagnostic evaluation of the hypoglossal nerve. *Arch Phys Med Rehabil.* 1984;65:633.
2. Redmond MD, DiBenedetto M. Hypoglossal nerve conduction in normal subjects. *Muscle Nerve.* 1988;11:447–452.

Ilioinguinal Nerve Conduction

1. Ellis RJ, Ceisse H, Holub BA, et al. Ilioinguinal nerve conduction. *Muscle Nerve.* 1992;15:1195.

Intercostal Nerve Conduction

1. Caldwell JW, Crane CR, Boland GL. Determinations of intercostal motor conduction time in diagnosis of nerve root compression. *Arch Phys Med Rehabil.* 1968;49:515–518.
2. Pradhan S, Taly A. Intercostal nerve conduction study in man. *J Neurol Neurosurg Psychiatry.* 1989;52:763–766.
3. Carls G, Ziemann U, Kunkel M, Reimers CD. Electrical and magnetic stimulation of the intercostal nerves: a comparative study. *Electromyogr Clin Neurophysiol.* 1997;37(8):509–512.

Lateral Cutaneous Sensory Nerve of the Calf

1. Campagnolo DI, Romello MA, Park YI, et al. Technique for studying conduction in the lateral cutaneous nerve of calf. *Muscle Nerve.* 2000;23:1277–1279.
2. Lee HJ, Bach HJ, DeLisa JA. Lateral dorsal cutaneous branch of the sural nerve: standardization in nerve conduction study. *Am J Phys Med Rehabil.* 1992;71(6):318–320.

Near-Nerve Needle Conduction Studies

1. Rosenfalck A. Early recognition of nerve disorders by near-nerve recordings of sensory nerve action potentials. *Muscle Nerve.* 1978;1(5):360–367.
2. Odabashi Z, Oh SJ, Claussen GC, Kim DS. New near-nerve needle nerve conduction technique: differentiating epicondylar from cubital tunnel ulnar neuropathy. *Muscle Nerve.* 1999;22:718–723.
3. Seo JH, Oh SJ. Near-nerve needle sensory conduction study of the medial calcaneal nerve: new method and report of four cases of medial calcaneal neuropathy. *Muscle Nerve.* 2002;26:654–658.

4. David WS, Doyle JJ. Segmental near nerve sensory conduction studies of the medial and lateral plantar nerve. *Electromyogr Clin Neurophysiol.* 1996;36:411–417.

5. Oh SJ, Kim HS, Ahmad BK. The near-nerve sensory nerve conduction in tarsal tunnel syndrome. *J Neurol Neurosurg Psychiatry.* 1985;48(10):999–1003.

6. Uluc K, Temucin CM, Ozdamar SE, et al. Near-nerve needle sensory and medial plantar nerve conduction studies in patients with small-fiber sensory neuropathy. *Eur J Neurol.* 2008;15(9):928–932.

7. Horowitz SH. Correlation of near-nerve sural conduction and quantified sensory testing in patients with diabetic neuropathy. *Muscle Nerve.* 1995;18(10):1202–1204.

8. Smith T. Near-nerve versus surface electrode recordings of sensory nerve conduction in patients with carpal tunnel syndrome. *Acta Neurol Scand.* 1998;98(4):280–282.

9. Deimel GW, Hurst RW, Sorenson EJ, Boon AJ. Ultrasound guided near nerve needle recording for the lateral femoral cutaneous sensory conduction study: does it increase reliability compared with surface recording? *Muscle Nerve.* 2013;47(2):274–276.

Cutaneous Silent Period

1. Lopergolo D, Isak B, Gabriele M, et al. Cutaneous silent period recordings in demyelinating and axonal polyneuropathies. *Clin Neurophysiol.* 2014;S1388–S2457. doi:10.1016/j.clinph.2014.11.013.

2. Onal MR, Ulas UH, Oz O, et al. Cutaneous silent period changes in type II diabetes mellitus patients with small fiber neuropathy. *Clin Neurophysiol.* 2010;121(5):714–718.

3. Han JK, Oh K, Kim BJ, et al. Cutaneous silent periods in patients with restless leg syndrome. *Clin Neurophysiol.* 2007;118(8):1705–1710.

4. Tiric-Campara M, Densislic M, Djelilovic-Vranic J, et al. Cutaneous silent period in the evaluation of small fibres. *Med Arch.* 2014;68(2):98–101.

5. Morkavuk G, Leventoglu A. Small fiber neuropathy associated with hyperlipidemia: utility of cutaneous silent periods and autonomic tests. *ISRN Neurol.* 2014;2014:579242.

6. Koytak PK, Isak B, Borucu D, et al. Assessment of symptomatic diabetic patients with normal nerve conduction studies: utility of cutaneous silent periods and autonomic tests. *Muscle Nerve.* 2011;43(3):317–323.

7. Floeter MK. Cutaneous silent periods. *Muscle Nerve.* 2003;28(4):391–401.

8. Sahin O, Yildiz S, Yildiz N. Cutaneous silent period in fibromyalgia. *Neurol Res.* 2011;33(4):339–343.

9. Isak B, Uluc K, Salcini C, et al. Neurophysiological approach to the complex organization of the spine: F-wave duration and cutaneous silent period in restless leg syndrome. *Clin Neurophysiol.* 2011;122(2):383–390.

Posterior Interosseous Sensory Response

1. Pelier-Cady MC, Raimbeau G, Saint Cast Y. Posterior interosseous nerve: sensory nerve conduction technique. Presented at the AAEM Annual Meeting; September 20, 1997.

Quadriceps Late Responses

1. Mongia SK. H reflex from quadriceps and gastrocnemius muscles. *Electromyography.* 1972;12:179–190.
2. Aiello I, Serra G, Rosati G, Tugnoli V. A quantitative method to analyze the H reflex latencies from vastus medialis muscle: normal values. *Electromyogr Clin Neurophysiol.* 1982;22:251–254.
3. Kameyama O, Hayes KC, Wolfe D. Methodological considerations contributing to variability of the quadriceps H-reflex. *Am J Phys Med Rehabil.* 1989;68:277–282.
4. Garland SJ, Gerilovsky L, Enoka RM. Association between muscle architecture and quadriceps femoris H-reflex. *Muscle Nerve.* 1994;17:581–592.
5. Wochnik-Dyjas D, Glazowski C, Niewiadoska M. The F-wave in the vastus lateralis M. and the segmental motor conduction times for L2/L4 motoneurons. *Electroencephalogr Clin Neurophysiol.* 1996;101:379–386.
6. Alrowayeh HN, Sabbahi MA. Vastus medialis H-reflex reliability during standing. *J Clin Neurophysiol.* 2006;23(1):79–84.
7. Doguet V, Jubeau M. Reliability of H-reflex in vastus lateralis and vastus medialis muscles during passive and active isometric conditions. *Eur J Appl Physiol.* 2014;114(12):2509–2519.

Radial Nerve Motor Conduction Study to the Triceps

1. Gassel MM. A test of nerve conduction to muscles of the shoulder girdle as an aid in the diagnosis of proximal neurogenic and muscular disease. *J Neurol Neurosurg Psychiatry.* 1964;27:200–205.

Repetitive Stimulation

1. Litchy WJ, Albers JW. *Repetitive Stimulation, An AAEM Workshop.* Rochester, MN: American Association of Electrodiagnostic Medicine; 1984.
2. Keesey JC. AAEM minimonograph #33: electrodiagnostic approach to defects of neuromuscular transmission. *Muscle Nerve.* 1989;12:613–626.
3. AAEM Quality Assurance Committee. American Association of Electrodiagnostic Medicine. Literature review of the usefulness of repetitive stimulation and single fiber EMG in the electrodiagnostic evaluation of patients

with suspected myasthenia gravis or Lambert-Eaton myasthenic syndrome. *Muscle Nerve.* 2001;24(9):1239–1247.

4. AAEM Quality Assurance Committee. American Association of Electrodiagnostic Medicine. Practice parameter for repetitive nerve stimulation and single fiber EMG evaluation of adults with suspected myasthenia gravis or Lambert-Eaton myasthenic syndrome: summary statement. *Muscle Nerve.* 2001;24(9):1236–1238.

Trigeminal Motor Nerve Conduction

1. Dillingham TR, Spellman NT, Chang AS. Trigeminal motor nerve conduction: deep temporal and mylohyoid nerves. *Muscle Nerve.* 1996;19:277–284.

2. Kimura J. Conduction abnormalities of the facial and trigeminal nerves in polyneuropathy. *Muscle Nerve.* 1982;5(9S):S139–S144.

Trigeminal Sensory Nerve Conduction

1. Raffaele R, Emery P, Palmeri A, et al. Sensory conduction velocity of the trigeminal nerve. *Electromyogr Clin Neurophysiol.* 1987;27:115–117.

2. Jandolo B, Gessini L, Pietrangeli A. Conduction velocity in human supraorbital nerve. *Eur Neurol.* 1981;20(5):421–423.

ANOMALOUS INNERVATION PATTERNS

INTRODUCTION

Anomalies of the peripheral nervous system occur commonly and knowledge of the most common of these is important to perform nerve conduction studies (NCS) and interpret the results. Lack of awareness of anomalous innervation will result in interpretation of the NCS that may lead to inappropriate conclusions (1). Anomalous innervation due to a median to ulnar (Martin–Gruber) anastomosis in the forearm is common. It is present in up to 30% of forearms normally and of those 68% can be bilateral (1,2). One or more of the first dorsal interossei (FDI), adductor pollicis, flexor pollicis, and abductor digiti minimi (ADM) can be supplied by fibers that originate from the median nerve (1,2). When present in a patient with carpal tunnel syndrome, it may cause confusion (3–6). For instance, a complete block of the median nerve to wrist stimulation may seem to be reversed on elbow stimulation. Martin–Gruber anastomosis (MGA) should be suspected if the median motor amplitude is larger on elbow stimulation than on wrist stimulation, and in persons with median nerve slowing across the wrist who have a higher than normal conduction velocity across the forearm. It should also be suspected if proximal (but not distal) median nerve stimulation results in an initially positive deflection.

MGA can usually be confirmed by repositioning the active electrode to the first dorsal interosseous muscle. Stimulation of the median nerve at the elbow, but not the wrist, results in a negative deflection. Stimulation at the elbow should also result in a significantly larger amplitude response than with wrist stimulation (1,3,5,7,8). An accurate forearm conduction velocity cannot be calculated in the person with carpal tunnel syndrome and an MGA.

Recognize MGA by the following possibilities:

1. Routine ulnar motor study recording over the ADM: pseudo-conduction block between wrist and below elbow (BE).
2. Routine ulnar motor study recording over the ADM: pseudo-conduction block between BE and above elbow (AE): this is the proximal MGA.
3. Ulnar nerve motor study recording over the FDI: pseudo-conduction block between wrist and BE.
4. Routine median motor study recording over the APB: increased compound muscle action potential (CMAP) amplitude proximally.
5. MGA + CTS: positive proximal dip and facetiously fast conduction velocity (1,5,7,8).

Note: Normal temporal dispersion: There can be up to a 10% drop in amplitude between different sites of stimulation.

Possibilities discussed in detail:

Routine ulnar nerve motor study recording from ADM—pseudo-conduction block between wrist and BE sites:

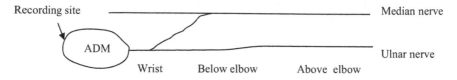

Recording site — Median nerve

ADM

Wrist   Below elbow   Above elbow

Ulnar nerve

NCS waveforms show the positive dip at median wrist and median elbow while recording at ADM

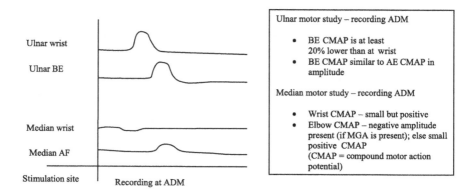

Ulnar wrist

Ulnar BE

Median wrist

Median AF

Stimulation site   Recording at ADM

Ulnar motor study – recording ADM

- BE CMAP is at least 20% lower than at wrist
- BE CMAP similar to AE CMAP in amplitude

Median motor study – recording ADM

- Wrist CMAP – small but positive
- Elbow CMAP – negative amplitude present (if MGA is present); else small positive CMAP (CMAP = compound motor action potential)

Possible differential diagnosis:
1. Excess stimulation of ulnar nerve at wrist resulting in costimulation of median nerve.
2. Submaximal stimulation of ulnar nerve at the BE site.
3. Conduction block in the ulnar nerve between wrist and BE.
4. MGA crossing fibers innervate ADM.

Routine ulnar nerve motor recording from ADM: pseudo-conduction block between BE and AE (proximal MGA):

Section of arm showing crossover of median fibers to ulnar between AE and BE

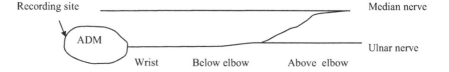

Recording site — Median nerve

ADM

Wrist   Below elbow   Above elbow

Ulnar nerve

NCS waveform with stimulation of ulnar and median motor nerves while recording at ADM

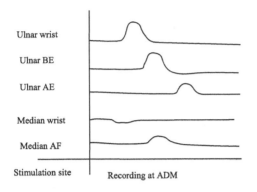

Ulnar wrist

Ulnar BE

Ulnar AE

Median wrist

Median AF

Stimulation site | Recording at ADM

Ulnar nerve motor – recording ADM

- AE CMAP is much smaller in amplitude as compared to BE CMAP
- Imitates conduction block between BE and AE
- Therefore mimics ulnar neuropathy at elbow

Median nerve motor – recording ADM

- Wrist CMAP – small but positive
- Elbow CMAP – negative amplitude (if MGA is present); else small positive CMAP

Ulnar nerve motor recording from first dorsal interosseus: Pseudo-conduction block between wrist and BE sites: (Most common MGA)

Record over FDI, fibers cross from median to ulnar nerve

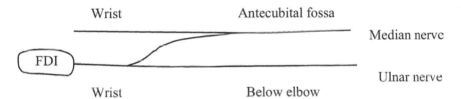

Wrist — Antecubital fossa

Median nerve

FDI

Ulnar nerve

Wrist — Below elbow

NCS waveform with ulnar stimulation at wrist and BE (drop in BE)

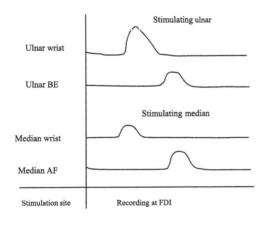

Stimulating ulnar

Ulnar wrist

Ulnar BE

Stimulating median

Median wrist

Median AF

Stimulation site | Recording at FDI

Ulnar nerve motor – recording FDI

- BE CMAP much lower than wrist
- Imitates conduction block between wrist and BE

Median nerve motor – recording FDI

- AF CMAP much higher than wrist

Other reasons to record over the FDI are:
1. Investigation of a deep palmar motor branch ulnar nerve.
2. Evaluation of a suspected ulnar neuropathy at elbow.

Routine median NCS recording from ABP—increased CMAP amplitude proximally:

MGA is to ulnar innervated thenar muscles, for example, adductor pollicis, deep head of FPB

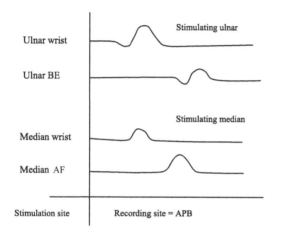

Differential diagnosis of the above pattern of recordings:
1. Submaximal stimulation of the median nerve at the wrist
2. Excessive stimulation of the median nerve at the antecubital fossa causing costimulation of the ulnar nerve
3. MGA with crossing fibers innervating the thenar eminence

MGA and CTS present concurrently

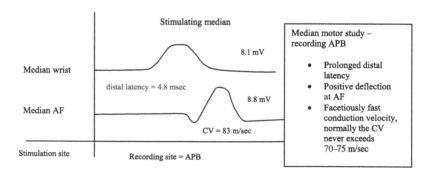

ACCESSORY DEEP FIBULAR NERVE

The accessory deep fibular nerve is the most common anomalous innervation of the lower extremity. It is a branch of the superficial fibular nerve that supplies the lateral portion of the extensor digitorum brevis (EDB) muscle (9–11). The nerve courses behind the lateral malleolus and can be stimulated there. It is present in up to 28% of individuals and when present 78% of relatives can also have the anomaly (1,9,12). When preforming fibular NCS the amplitude of the EDB with ankle stimulation should be 90%–120% of the amplitude obtained with stimulation at the knee. The accessory deep fibular nerve should be considered if this amplitude relationship does not exist and the amplitude obtained at the ankle is smaller (12–15).

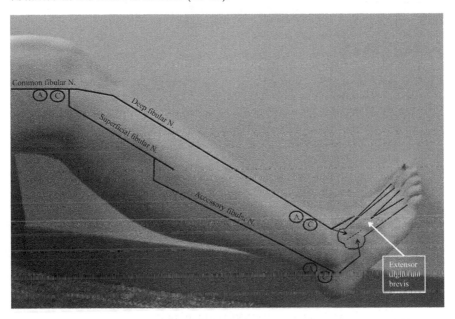

Incomplete accessory deep fibular nerve:

Sites	Rec Site	Resp	Lat ms	Amp mV	Rel Amp %
1. Ankle	EDB		3.6	0.7	-
2. FibHead	EDB		9.7	3.0	-
3. Knee	EDB				

Ankle 1

20 ms 2 mV 64 mA

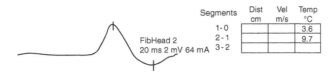

FibHead 2
20 ms 2 mV 64 mA

Segments	Dist cm	Vel m/s	Temp °C
1-0			3.6
2-1			9.7
3-2			

Deep fibular nerve without accessory deep fibular nerve:

Sites	Rec Site	Resp	Lat ms	Amp mV	Rel Amp %
1. Ankle	EDB		3.3	4.1	-
2. FibHead	EDB		9.7	3.7	-
3. Knee	EDB				

Ankle 1
20 ms 2 mV 64 mA

Segments	Dist cm	Vel m/s	Temp °C
1 - 0			
2 - 1	34	53	
3 - 2			

FibHead 2
20 ms 2 mV 64 mA

REFERENCES

1. Gutmann L. AAEM minimonograph #2: important anomalous innervations of the extremities. *Muscle Nerve.* 1993;16:339–347.

2. Rodriguez-Niedenführ M, Vazquez T, Parkin I, et al. Martin Gruber anastomosis revisited. *Clin Anat.* 2002;15(2):129–134.

3. van Dijk JG, Bouma PA. Recognition of the Martin-Gruber anastomosis. *Muscle Nerve.* 1997;20(7):887–889.

4. Wilbourn AJ, Lambert EH. The forearm median to ulnar nerve communication, electrodiagnostic aspects. *Neurology.* 1976;26, 368.

5. Rubin DI, Dimberg EL. Martin-Gruber anastomosis and carpal tunnel syndrome: morphologic clues to identification. *Muscle Nerve.* 2010;42(3):457–458. (Erratum in: *Muscle Nerve.* 2011;43(4):623.)

6. Lesser EA, Venkatesh S, Preston DC, Logigian EL. Stimulation distal to the lesion in patients with carpal tunnel syndrome. *Muscle Nerve.* 1995;18:503–507.

7. Sander HW, Quinto C, Chokroverty S. Median-ulnar anastomosis to thenar, hypothenar, and first dorsal interosseous muscles: collision technique confirmation. *Muscle Nerve.* 1997;20(11):1460–1462.

8. Sun SF, Streib EW. Martin-Gruber anastomosis: electromyographic studies. *Electromyogr clin Neurophysiol.* 1983;23:271–285.

9. Mathis S, Ciron J, du Boisguéheneuc F, et al. Study of accessory deep peroneal nerve motor conduction in a population of healthy subjects. *Neurophys Clin.* 2011;41(1):214–215.

10. Prakash, Bhardwaj AK, Singh DK, et al. Anatomic variations of superficial peroneal nerve: clinical implications of a cadaver study. *Ital J Anat Embryol.* 2010;115(3):223–228.

11. Ubogu EE. Complete innervation of extensor digitorum brevis by accessory peroneal nerve. *Neuromuscul Disord.* 2005;15(8):562–564.

12. Rayegani SM, Daneshtalab E, Bahrami MH, et al. Prevalence of accessory deep peroneal nerve in referred patients to an electrodiagnostic medicine clinic. *J Brachial Plex Peripher Nerve Inj*. 2011;6:3.

13. Marciniak C, Armon C, Wilson J, Miller R. Practice parameter: utility of electrodiagnostic techniques in evaluating patients with suspected peroneal neuropathy: an evidence based review. *Muscle Nerve*. 2005;31(4):520–527.

14. Posa HNRM. Nerve conduction studies of the medial branch of deep peroneal nerve. *Muscle Nerve*. 1990;13:862.

15. Kayal R, Katirji B. In atypical deep peroneal neuropathy in the setting of an accessory deep peroneal nerve. *Muscle Nerve*. 2009:4(2):313–315.

APPENDIX 2

BMI TABLES

Body Mass Index (BMI—kg/m²)

Metric Calculation												
Height (cm)	Weight (kg)											
	45	**50**	**55**	**60**	**65**	**70**	**75**	**80**	**85**	**90**	**95**	**100**
150	20	22	24	27	29	31	33	36	38	40	42	44
160	18	20	21	23	25	27	29	31	33	35	37	39
170	16	17	19	21	22	24	26	28	29	31	33	35
180	14	15	17	19	20	22	23	25	26	28	29	31
190	12	14	15	17	18	19	21	22	24	25	26	28
200	11	13	14	15	16	18	19	20	21	23	24	25

English Calculation

Height (in)	110	115	120	125	130	135	140	145	150	155	160	165	170	175	180	185	190	195	200	205	210	215	220	225	230	235
														Weight (lbs)											
5'0"	21	22	23	24	25	26	27	28	29	30	31	32	33	34	35	36	37	38	39	40	41	42	43	44	45	46
5'1"	21	22	23	24	25	26	26	27	28	29	30	31	32	33	34	35	36	37	38	39	40	41	42	43	43	44
5'2"	20	21	22	23	24	25	26	27	27	28	29	30	31	32	33	34	35	36	37	37	38	39	40	41	42	43
5'3"	19	20	21	22	23	24	25	26	27	27	28	29	30	31	32	33	34	35	35	36	37	38	39	40	41	42
5'4"	19	20	21	21	22	23	24	25	26	27	27	28	29	30	31	32	33	33	34	35	36	37	38	39	39	40
5'5"	18	19	20	21	22	22	23	24	25	26	27	27	28	29	30	31	32	32	33	34	35	36	37	37	38	39
5'6"	18	19	19	20	21	22	23	23	24	25	26	27	27	28	29	30	31	31	32	33	34	35	36	36	37	38
5'7"	17	18	19	20	20	21	22	23	23	24	25	26	27	27	28	29	30	31	31	32	33	34	34	35	36	37
5'8"	17	17	18	19	20	21	21	22	23	24	24	25	26	27	27	28	29	30	30	31	32	33	33	34	35	36
5'9"	16	17	18	18	19	20	21	21	22	23	24	24	25	26	27	27	28	29	30	30	31	32	32	33	34	35
5'10"	16	16	17	18	19	19	20	21	22	22	23	24	24	25	26	27	27	28	29	29	30	31	32	32	33	34
5'11"	15	16	17	17	18	19	20	20	21	22	22	23	24	24	25	26	27	27	28	29	29	30	31	31	32	33
6'0"	15	16	16	17	18	18	19	20	20	21	22	22	23	24	24	25	26	26	27	28	28	29	30	31	31	32
6'1"	15	15	16	16	17	18	18	19	20	20	21	22	22	23	24	24	25	26	26	27	28	28	29	30	30	31
6'2"	14	15	15	16	17	17	18	19	19	20	21	21	22	22	23	24	24	25	26	26	27	28	28	29	30	30
6'3"	14	14	15	16	16	17	17	18	19	19	20	21	21	22	22	23	24	24	25	26	26	27	27	28	29	29
6'4"	13	14	15	15	16	16	17	18	18	19	19	20	21	21	22	23	23	24	24	25	26	26	27	27	28	29

INDEX

Note: Boldface numbers indicate illustrations.

Lightning Source UK Ltd.
Milton Keynes UK
UKOW06f1832310317

298064UK00008B/125/P